STUDIES IN CULTURE & COMMUNICATION

Martin S. Dworkin, General Editor

The series is devoted to education in its most comprehensive meaning, embracing the activities of formal instruction and learning carried on in schools, and all the forces of social influence upon the development and behavior of individuals and groups. Drawing upon a broad range of literatures, in many languages, the series presents new and rediscovered works, focusing closely on critical studies of the arts, educational implications of courses of thought and behavior, and tactics and instruments of profession and persuasion. No partiality of doctrine or expression is intended or imposed, the selections following a sovereign purpose to stimulate and inform the continuing critique of ideas, values, and modes of communication that is the growing tissue of education, and the perennial flowering of culture.

JEFFERSONIANISM AND THE AMERICAN NOVEL
Howard Mumford Jones

MODERN AESTHETICS: AN HISTORICAL INTRODUCTION
The Earl of Listowel

JEFFERSONIANISM

AND THE

AMERICAN NOVEL

HOWARD MUMFORD JONES

PS 371
.J 77

TEACHERS COLLEGE PRESS
Teachers College, Columbia University
New York

To

Richard M. Ludwig

who bears with my infirmities

GENERAL EDITOR'S FOREWORD

FICTION AND TEACHING

THAT fiction argues and teaches, as well as entertains, is an historic determination—a landmark in the development of critical consciousness, of the individual and social processes of self-awareness and judgment that Bruno Snell aptly names "The Discovery of the Mind." Indeed, it is at the point of criticism of fiction, of the mythological narratives of the traditional, sacred poetic literature that much of Western systematic philosophy—most notably the concerns of ethics and education—begins in ancient Greece. And it is at this point of classical convergences that there occurs some of the most mordantly radical consideration of the beliefs and ways of living of any age. For it is here, where the free imaginings of artists meet the reaching desires of audiences, that there may be the most faithful revelations of the ethos of a people. Thus, insofar as the criticism of fiction involves criticism of the popular imagination in its topical enthusiasms, it may be the critic, despite any ostensible conservatism, who most truly challenges the conventional spirit and behavior of his time; while the story teller, for all the personified indictments and dramatized objections of his narratives, as conservator of his own popularity may be able at best to prepare the grounds for critical understanding and judgment. At worst, to be sure, his stories may subvert criticism as well as change, placating the very dissatisfactions they expose in providing a catharsis of entertainment.

This is not to deny the place of fiction in affecting action, as in preparing revolutions or encouraging progress, but to remind that stories, to remain stories, must have their limits; and that claims for their bearing on events must comprehend the processes whereby the interior reality of the imagination achieves exterior reality, in all the infinite variety of individual behavior. If fiction teaches, it is reality that learns. And this educational relationship implies those mutual dependencies and responsibilities that led the first philosophers of education to caution against the unbridled imaginings of the narrative and dramatic poets. Says the Athenian Stranger (an idealization of the aged Plato himself?) in the *Laws,* associating the popular singers and playwrights with the philosopher-lawgivers of the city to be established: ". . . we are composers of the same things as yourselves, rivals of yours as artists and actors of the fairest drama, which, as our hope is, true law, and it alone, is by nature competent to complete." * This "fairest drama," of course, is the life of government—*self*-government in the truly Greek and essentially humanistic meaning of the operative analogy of polity and citizen, of the organic unity of political and moral life. And the "true law" is not any body of precepts or statutes, conceived by vested authority and enforced by power, but, as Socrates had argued earlier, the principles of virtuous, harmonious living to be individually discovered and applied in reasoned inquiry, itself the way and essential spirit of the good life.

To construe fiction and philosophy simply as opposites is to miss the point—in course perpetuating hoary, simplistic metaphors of "art" versus "intellect," "feeling" versus "reason." These have passed as contrarieties of subsistent principles for so long as to take on considerable historical reality; although to so separate the inseparable, organismic mutuality of human functions and characteristics is patent reification and patently absurd—except in limited, formal reductive analysis. Even historically, it is relevant to note that the momentous counterposition in Parmenides, of the beginnings of systematic, "philosophical" reasoning, and traditional cosmogonic mythologizing, occurs within a single work—of poetry! And, indeed, the very formulations of Plato, so long and so easily interpreted as condemning all works of imagination, and especially poetry and fiction, appear in context of some of the most sublimely imaginative dialogues ever created. The issue, then, is not that of philosophy as *non*poetry or *non*fiction, opposing poetry or fiction as *non*philosophy. Such distinctions cannot withstand extended analysis of the nature and relationship of "reason" and "imagination," and do too much violence too

---

* vii. 817. Trans. R. G. Bury, Loeb Classical Library (Cambridge, Mass., 1926), Vol. II, p. 99.

easily to too many works, from the pre-Socratics and Plato to Voltaire, Rousseau, Goethe, Dostoyevsky, Santayana, Eliot, Sartre, and Camus. What humanists, at least since Democritus and Socrates, have said all along is that all fictions philosophize; all songs and stories, dramas, and other entertainments provide instruction; and the governance of self and of society is at stake at the point of judgment.

To say any less is to argue the irrelevance of the arts in the lives of men and societies. This position, to be sure, is one to which ideologues of "art for the sake of art" are ineluctably committed, despite their own mis-understandings of their fervent advocacies in the name of freedom of expression and experience. Even the deliberate search for irrelevance must carry banners in the competing parades of an era and is doomed to significance among the passing schools and movements—if only the significance of irresponsibility.

The assertion that the arts have civic responsibilities, however, does accentuate the dual problem of censorship and propaganda, already implicit in the consideration of education itself. In the endless struggle for freedom, it is the very forces of expression and enlightenment that are most susceptible of usurpation by tyrannical intentions—no matter how sentimentally revolutionist and progressive. But the most insidious tyrannies are those that are self-imposed under illusions of liberation from all restriction—recalling Goethe's warning, at the height of the Enlightenment, of the destructiveness of whatever emancipates the spirit without affording self-control.* Indeed, it is in pursuing the intricate relationships of fiction and teaching, of art and education, that there is clearest recognition of the persistent actuality of some kind of control over whatever is made public in whatever form. The nature of such control, in fact, may distinguish most sharply the formal and informal modes of education in a society: the curricular processes of teaching and learning in constituted schools and the germinal inspirations and ex-periences of the enveloping culture. And, *a fortiori,* it is in effecting such control as self-control, toward ends of individual fulfillment and social justice, that the schools and the arts serve the true purposes of freedom.

In his *Jeffersonianism and the American Novel,* Howard Mumford Jones recalls fiction to civic responsibility, arguing the essential citizen-ship of letters at a time of profound, if not fatal disorientation. Not only do artists, specifically novelists, manifest their own alienation—as, in-deed, may be vital to the meaning and integrity of their art. But, insofar

---

* *"Alles, was unsern Geist befreit, ohne uns die Herrschaft über uns selbst zu geben, ist verderblich."* In *Sprüche in Prosa, Maximen und Reflexionen,* I.

as they profess art as the salvationary mode for all living, they, and their myriad epigones in the cultural industries, in effect make propaganda for irrationalism as the only true conduct, and for alienation as the basis of society. Such principles may be spiritually corrosive, as well as philosophically and sociologically absurd. Nevertheless, they may achieve immense operational force in the lives of hordes of people, practicing pathetic, dangerous rituals of "artistic" dislocation on the edges of sanity and civic permissiveness. Let there be no comfort here for philistine crusaders against artists as arrant maniacs or sinful voluptuaries. But let there be no sustenance, as well, for those who do sin against man in making art do less than the raising of man above himself.

Professor Jones chooses to measure the course of fiction in America against the developing meaning of Jeffersonian ideas and influences. In so doing, he recurs to concerns that are classical, as discussed above, in the sense of being fundamental as well as historical, perennial as well as immediately topical. The evocation of Jeffersonianism is not of an encrusted orthodoxy, but of a truly revolutionary spirit, culminating the noblest works and thoughts of the humanistic tradition, in advancing the primal aspirations of man toward enlightenment and responsible self-government. The indictment of fiction not only brings the popular imagination to judgment according to its own highest ideals, but asseverates the responsibilities of literary artists as spokesmen and teachers, and as citizens of the republic forever coming into being, according to their own professions of humane values and spiritual commitment. This is as criticism should do, and no disagreement with particular opinions of books or ideas need diminish the illuminations and recreative pleasures of the argument.

In his lecture on "The Novel of Man," delivered at the Brussels World's Fair in 1958, Georges Simenon spoke as the writer of fiction fully aware of what is always asked of fiction: "The man of today does not yet know which image of himself to choose, and a whole generation is in quest of its hero." That the hero turns out to be man himself, in his highest virtue and potentiality, and in the face of all weakness, evil, and catastrophe, is Simenon's hope—as it is, in Professor Jones's view, the Jeffersonian ideal for the novelist. That the image always become real is the eternal task of teaching, made no less vital for its endless disappointment, and no less demanding for its endless glory.

Martin S. Dworkin

New York City
September, 1966

PREFACE

A book by a friend of mine begins: "This is a working paper. If it isn't, I don't know when it stopped being one."

This book is a working paper on the relation between what is thought of as the American way and what we think of as the American novel. It is not an inquiry into the aesthetics of the American novel, nor into the development of the American novel, nor into the relation of the American novel to any other sort of novel in any other country. It is an inquiry into what seems to me a grave central problem in contemporary culture: in what manner and to what degree has the American novel in the last two centuries supported or denied the current assumption that ideal life in America presupposes what we talk about sometimes as democracy and sometimes as Jeffersonian democracy?

To those of us who are disturbed by a good many irrational tendencies in American life the American novel offers cold comfort. Our discomfort does not arise from the assumption that the nineteenth-century novel in the United States was, in the main, "wholesome," and the twentieth century has been, or is becoming, more and more "decadent," though that position has been taken by some interpreters. It arises rather from the disappearance from American fiction—or if not disappearance, then, certainly, the portentous weakening—of the concept of the adult American as a being capable of both rational and moral choice. Upon this assumption, despite depth psychology, and hidden persuaders, and fashionable current criticism, and smart teaching in classrooms about contemporary writing, this republic rests; and in proportion as this assumption is weakened by the most powerful form of imaginative literature among us, the foundation of the republic is shaken. Either the bases of the republic must be philosophically reshaped; or modern teaching and modern criticism must find some way simultaneously to protect the autonomy of art and to warn readers that art may conceivably betray the political republic. It may betray the political republic by naïvely assuming that a primary duty of the political republic is to protect the republic of letters but that it is no primary duty of the republic of letters to protect the health and safety of the political republic.

I am immensely indebted to Lawrence A. Cremin for suggesting that this theme has educational implications; and to the Center for Advanced Study in the Behavioral Sciences for giving me an opportunity to work at this manuscript. I am grateful also to the Guggenheim Foundation for giving me the opportunity to put the book into shape.

Some part of this study was delivered as the annual Stephen S. Wise lecture at the Hebrew Union College–Jewish Institute of Religion at Los Angeles.

Howard Mumford Jones

Harvard University

CONTENTS

CHAPTER I

THE PROBLEM

i

In 1909 Herbert Croly published *The Promise of American Life,* a basic book for understanding liberalism, particularly American liberalism in the days of Teddy Roosevelt, Taft, and Woodrow Wilson, and an interpretation that, though dated in some particulars, is still relevant and illuminating. Croly analyzed the operations of two great political traditions in American history—that of Hamilton, which was dedicated to liberty, and that of Jefferson, which was dedicated to equality. Frankly of Hamilton's school, in this study he nevertheless demanded the correction of Hamiltonian rigor by Jeffersonian doctrine. He wavered in his interpretation of Jefferson, for, though he came out in favor of the enrichment of the individual life, he said that Jefferson's political system was intended for the benefit only of average people, an interpretation which, to anybody who has studied Jefferson's philosophy of public education, is nonsense. But in fact Croly took over the Jeffersonian concepts of public responsibility for education and of educational responsibility for the commonweal.

Hamilton, said Croly, realized that "genuine liberty . . . could be protected only by an energetic and clear-sighted central government, and . . . could be fertilized only by the efficient national organization of American activities." But the central government was growing too big and too forgetful of individual lives, and Hamiltonian theory had also created great centers of power outside government. Croly devoted a good many pages to an ironical analysis of the place in American society of the business specialist, the political specialist, the labor specialist, and the legal specialist, by which terms he meant the millionaire, the political boss, the labor-union leader, and the corporation lawyer. If he spoke about Hamilton's principle of national responsibility and Jefferson's principle of national irresponsibility, he was not content to leave it at that. Out of this Hegelian thesis and antithesis he wanted to derive a synthesis, a fusion of Hamiltonian liberty and Jeffersonian equality, or, more specifically, he wanted to throw the power of the central government in the direction of identifying individual excellence and enriching the lives of ordinary Americans.

At the time he was writing he thought most Americans had taken both laissez-faire liberty and democratic equality for granted. But these were not interchangeable terms. Croly anticipated much contemporary comment about the impoverishment of the individual life in the United States and much of our contemporary quest for ways of enriching the intellectual, moral, and aesthetic dimensions of that life. Americans should realize that it is the responsibility of government, conceived as the Hamilton aegis for the protection of liberties, to move actively in the direction of Jeffersonian individualism.

> The great lesson of American political experience . . . is rather that of interdependence than of incompatibility between the efficient national organization and a group of radical democratic institutions and ideals; and the meaning of this lesson has been obscured because the Federal organization has not been constituted in a sufficiently democratic spirit.

He came to refer to the United States as a democracy. Democracy must, he said,

> . . . cease to be a democracy of indiscriminate individualism, and become one of selected individuals who are obliged constantly to justify their selection; and its members must be united . . . by a sense of joint responsibility for the success of their political and social ideal.

This, clearly, is the Jeffersonian doctrine of a natural aristocracy, and here, implicitly, is the concept of democracy as government resting upon the consent of the governed.

In thus remaking American life, education, Croly argued, was a central force, or should be. Democratic education must deal justly with both individualism and excellence. Individuality, he said, cannot be dissociated from the pursuit of a disinterested object,* the Americans must give up their naïve faith in education as natural magic and must come to realize that education cannot offer Americans "a sufficiently complete chance of self-expression until the American nation has earnestly undertaken and measurably achieved the realization of its collective purpose." That purpose was, and is, two-fold: to substantiate the rational responsibility of the citizen for the democratic state; and to identify and enrich individual excellence without thereby impoverishing the lives of the sad average. On his very last page Croly quoted from the chapter on "Democracy" in George Santayana's *The Life of Reason: Reason in Society,* published four years earlier. Santayana had written:

> For such excellence to grow general mankind must be notably transformed. If a noble and civilised democracy is to subsist, the common citizen must be something of a saint and something of a hero. We see therefore how justly flattering and profound, and at the same time how ominous, was Montesquieu's saying that the principle of democracy is virtue.

I add parenthetically that Santayana's chapter is one of the best brief discussions of the kinds and problems of social and political democracy anywhere in print.

More than fifty years have passed since Croly's book was published. If *The Promise of American Life* could not anticipate two world wars, the rise of fascism, and the spread of communism, it was nevertheless in many ways a prophetical book. It is true that Croly over-estimated the future grip of a laissez-faire philosophy on the American people and underestimated the growth in the scope and authority of the central government. Concentrations of financial and industrial power which he described are possibly kept under severer control nowadays than when Teddy Roosevelt was trust-busting. The welfare state, which he dimly outlined, if it has increased the dead level of dead commonplace, has likewise enriched American health and comfort and prolonged American life. Croly did not always define what he meant by generalities like "experimental collective action" as the aim of a modernized democracy, so that he can on occasion justly be charged with cloudy thinking. Nevertheless, his analysis is still in many ways valid; and three important com-

---

* In view of the contemporary misuse of this word as meaning "lacking in interest" or "having no interest for me," I trust it is not pettish to remark that Croly uses "disinterested" in its proper sense.

ponents of his analysis are especially significant today. These are his identification of the American state, despite his pro-Hamilton leanings, with democracy in the Jeffersonian sense; his belief in a necessary and vital connection between democracy and education, both institutional and individualized; and his return upon the Jeffersonian concept of rational individualism because he thought that Hamiltonian power concentration had gone too far in the name of liberty and was destroying the very individual liberties it was supposed to nourish and protect.

Thirty years after the publication of Croly's book another volume by another liberal appeared, Archibald MacLeish's poem, *America Was Promises*. The change in temporal perspective is important. Croly located American promise in the future; MacLeish looked back upon it. This backward look did not mean that MacLeish was less liberal or less devoted than Croly, it meant only that in his passionate desire for American action against the fascist powers MacLeish could not find the support he wanted among his contemporaries and had to turn to Jefferson, to John Adams, and to Tom Paine for the true quintessence of American faith. It is interesting to note that this poet of American history, in the "Empire-Builders" section of his *Frescoes for Mr. Rockefeller's City* (1933), had versified a letter from Meriwether Lewis to President Jefferson about the Lewis and Clark expedition, and that, as Librarian of Congress, he played a central part in the ceremonies celebrating the dedication of the Jefferson Memorial in Washington in 1943.

There are three great presidential memorials in the national capital, commemorating Washington, Lincoln, and Jefferson, dedicated in 1884, 1922, and 1943 respectively. There is no equally impressive memorial to Alexander Hamilton. The movement in American values from the United States under Chester A. Arthur to the United States under Franklin D. Roosevelt is illuminating: Jefferson's name acquires more and more glamor, Hamilton's name retains respect only. The war against the Axis states was understood to be a war that would determine whether a Jeffersonian democracy rather than a Hamiltonian timocracy could survive; and though the country survives under a Hamiltonian central government far more penetrating and powerful than anything Croly ever dreamed, in common thought ours is now a Jeffersonian democratic republic. I call it a republic because that is still its form of government, however altered from the government of Jefferson's time. I call it democratic because, except for a few vestigial remnants like the electoral college and the disappearing poll-tax, power now lies wholly in the hands of the people save in a few states still voting for Jefferson Davis. And I call it Jeffersonian because the words we use to talk about the United

States as a political and cultural entity are words that, whatever their present meaning, descend from the world of Thomas Jefferson. Debate rages among philosophers, political scientists, psychologists, and plain men about the meanings of these words, but we continue to use them in political life, in our courts, and in general American speech. In public life, for example, the civil rights and the desegregation movements, in the courts the test of sanity as the ability to distinguish right from wrong (the "moral sense"), in ordinary speech such constructions as "You ought to know better," "It's logical, isn't it?" and "I wouldn't trust him from here to there"—expressions assuming a moral sense or a rational faculty —are, so to speak, pure Jeffersonianism.

ii

Contemporary Americans, then, think of themselves, their culture, and their country, however vaguely, in Jeffersonian terms and have been encouraged to do so by commentators of the type of Croly and Archibald MacLeish. Moreover, ever since John Dewey, American educational philosophy has had a strong Jeffersonian bias. Democracy is to begin in the schoolroom. Under-privileged children are to have such special attention (another Jeffersonian idea) as will make them equal citizens in an egalitarian state, or at least do as much for them in this direction as science and pedagogy can accomplish. Segregation in the schools has been struck down because it makes for inequality. Mental tests and measurements are supposed not merely to indicate the potentials of young Americans but also to help us sort out the leading spirits of tomorrow. Self-help in the way of adult education (an old nineteenth-century concept) has received new impetus, both commercial and otherwise. Croly's demands for both institutional education and the education through the mere act of living which the Germans call in a general sense *Bildung* are, in a way, being fulfilled.

It must be remembered that for Croly the second of these concepts in a democratic state is quite as important as the first. The whole tenor of American life, he thought, should be oriented to a Jeffersonian aim. Writing before radio and television had invaded American homes and during the infancy of the moving pictures, he nevertheless argues that the arts and sciences, that general culture should have an essential role in enriching individual lives and in educating the future leaders of a progressive nation. In a democratic society a literate citizenry is an absolute necessity, but literacy means more than the bare ability to read and write, it means a capacity to deal with ideas, to judge conduct. If in Montesquieu's words virtue is an essential characteristic of a successful republic, is not virtue, is not duty, is not intelligence, is not responsible civic action a *sine qua non* in politics? and if these, or some of these, are necessary, how are they supported? how used? Are they made a part of life from day to day?

This is the age of the mass media, and we have had various studies of the movies, of radio, and of television as modern communication arts, and of the comics, murder stories, science fiction, popular magazines, popular music, and best-sellers. It must be confessed that most of these studies offer little encouragement to the proposition that in a democratic state the democratic arts now nourish a lively sense for duty and for civic virtue. And the situation has worsened since Croly wrote. Thus Mr. Gilbert Seldes, who in 1924 turned against the highbrows with humor and vigor when he wrote *The Seven Lively Arts* (1924)—his essay on Krazy Kat is a classic in this genre—when he came to publish *The Great Audience* (1950) a quarter of a century later, had grown pessimistic. The hucksters had come to dominate the field so completely, intelligence was being soothed and lulled. The mass media were, he felt, afraid to employ controversial figures, on the whole they shunned genuine public discussion, and they displayed less interest in the fortunes of the republic than they did in the fortunes of Madison Avenue.

In 1957 Bernard Rosenberg and David Manning White edited a big collection of analytical studies by specialists, entitled *Mass Culture: The Popular Arts in America,* and on the whole, to this reader at least, the studies do not encourage a belief in a movement toward a genuine Jeffersonian democracy. The editors, to be sure, reached opposite conclusions and quite honestly stated their points of difference. "There can be no doubt," said Mr. Rosenberg in his introductory remarks, "that the mass media present a major threat to man's autonomy." Man's autonomy is axiomatic in the Jeffersonian philosophy. Mr. White was more encouraging. He thought that the mass media offered unusual opportunities for choice to the American. On one evening, for example, the patron was offered a chance to choose between Godfrey's Talent Scouts show and the ballet of the Sadler's Wells Theater. Mr. White was eloquent on the sale of "classical" records, on the broadcasting of symphony and opera, on the sale of "good" books in paperback editions. And he liked the Sunday radio programs. All he said may be true, but that opera and ballet are piped into the American home (or apartment), that Bellow's *Adventures of Augie March* sold widely in paperback and but thinly as a hard-cover book, or that you can meet the press on television does not inevitably make for rationality, the strengthening of the moral sense, or civic responsibility. Confrontation on the "Meet the Press" program has its virtues, but these virtues do not resemble those evident in the Lincoln-Douglas debates. Playing Bartok's music over FM stations does nothing to make the younger generation understand that if they wish to influence public policy, sit-downs in courthouses or university buildings, however admirable their emotional intent, are not only not policy but also destroy the concept of a regular electoral process and ordinary representative government.

Among the arts, popular or otherwise, that of literature, however defined, deals more directly with ideas than does any other—which is not to be construed as meaning that painting, the dance, and architecture are unintelligent. We are perhaps too close to the moving pictures, radio, and television to judge their permanent effects, but literature has been with us a long time. Until the rise of the mass media, literature, particularly fiction, has been a powerful agency in shaping the American mind, the American sense of public and private virtue. It seems important to inquire, therefore, whether literature has helped or hindered the Jeffersonian philosophy. Have the American novelists been for or against the American state? What have been their basic concepts of human nature, not as art but as philosophy and psychology? What pictures do they give the American of the American as citizen? Do they believe in the moral faculty, or the moral sense, or, indeed, in moral principle as the founding fathers did? What is their attitude towards man considered as a rational being? Despite the library of books about Jefferson and about democracy in the twentieth century, few persons have made such inquiry, though it would seem to be an important inquiry, one fraught with omen for the future of the republic. What can we find out? Our findings, can we make any, should be important both for education in any sense and for democracy, however defined.

CHAPTER II

THE ELEMENTS OF FICTION

i

In examining the relation between the Jeffersonian view of man and the American novel I think we must begin by looking at the novel as a literary manifestation of American culture and then try, if we can, to arrive at some statement of what one means by Jeffersonianism. After that one can turn to the leading novelists of the nineteenth century, and conclude by analyzing some trends in fiction published since 1917. If one were concerned with the full impact of Jeffersonianism upon American writing one would have to deal with poetry from Philip Freneau to Robert Frost, with the theater from Royal Tyler's *The Contrast* to the latest confection by Tennessee Williams, and with writers of non-fictional prose as influential as Emerson and Thoreau, E. B. White and Walter Lippmann. I sacrifice the larger opportunity without regret.

There can be no doubt about the centrality of the novel in the literature of the American republic. Book lists illustrate this centrality. Fiction is the mainstay of our general publishing houses, and though the exceptional popularity of a Longfellow or a Robert Frost, of a James Whitcomb Riley or an Edgar Guest may make them valuable literary properties, the novel remains the backbone of general publishing. It was, of course, not always so. Lyle H. Wright, the leading authority on earlier American fiction, could find only 25 novels, however classified, by American authors, however defined, for the decade 1800 to 1809. But by the eighteen-forties these twenty-five had increased to 765. This number, however, is as nothing compared to our twentieth-century output. From 1900 to 1939, for example, we published 32,871 titles in fiction, and the next largest number of books—what are technically called juveniles, themselves often fictional—amounted to less than half the number of novels, or 14,536. If one selects a typical recent year—say, 1960—one finds that publishers brought out in that year 2,440 novels and 1,725 juveniles, whereas books of history in the twelve-month numbered a mere 197. In 1964 we published 3,261 volumes of fiction, 1,703 of them being "new" novels and 1,568 of them new editions. Paperback fiction in the same year amounted to 1,853 titles.

The power of this fiction in molding the American outlook is one of the most striking things about it. To Cooper we owe our principal myth concerning the American frontier. To Hawthorne we owe our principal myth concerning Puritan New England. To Harriet Beecher Stowe we owe our principal myth concerning slavery. To Henry James we owe our principal myth about American innocence and European corruption. To Sinclair Lewis we owe our principal myth about American business. In vain do historians tell us that the frontier, Puritanism, slavery, international society, and American business ethics were or are far more complex than they appear to be in the cases of Leatherstocking, Hester Prynne, Uncle Tom, Isabel Archer, and George Babbitt. Fiction creates its own patterns and stamps their image upon the American imagination.

Of course, the novel was a late starter in the literary race. Despite scholarly interest in forerunners like *The Power of Sympathy,* the novel did not come into its own until the decade of Jefferson's death, a truth that makes our inquiry the more interesting because Jeffersonian specialists have told us little about the influence of Jeffersonian ideas upon this literary form. Professor Daniel Boorstin in his *The Lost World of Thomas Jefferson* does not discuss Jeffersonianism in fiction, and Professor Merrill Peterson, in his admirable book on the Jeffersonian image, ignores the novel. Parenthetically, there are only a few novels about Jefferson. Our interest, however, is not in these but in the question whether this major American genre has in any way re-enforced or denied the Jeffersonian image of man.

ii

The inquiry faces two enormous primary difficulties—one created by the novel and one created by Jefferson. Let us begin with the novel. No one has ever successfully isolated or defined this elusive, yet potent literary type. We have had novels epistolary, autobiographical, historical, naturalistic, adventurous, and of the stream-of-consciousness persuasion. We have had tough novels and tender novels. We have had novels told in the first person and novels written from an omniscient point of view. We have had burlesque novels, *romans à clef*, novels as short as Stephen Crane's *Maggie* and as long as *The Naked and the Dead*. We have had novels out of which short stories have been carved, short stories that have developed into novels, novels that have turned into stage plays, and plays that have been altered into novels. The influence of Europe has been powerful, but so has the influence of Hollywood, of radio, and television. For Cooper the novel was a rational form; today the influence of non-rational psychology and of philosophies of pessimism and nescience seems prepotent. A single lapse from sexual propriety occasions the story of the first American novel; in contemporary fiction characters climb in and out of each other's beds or studio couches without embarrassment. No wonder the attempt of Webster's Dictionary to define this protean form is unsuccessful.

There one reads that the novel is "a lengthy fictitious narrative in prose having an almost unlimited range of subject-matter and varied techniques, which may contain one or more plots, and the treatment of which may range from photographic realism to highly imaginative themes." This is gallant but not helpful—in fact, it is not even accurate as far as it goes, and it does not go very far. A theme is not "treatment," a novel need not be in prose, length remains conveniently undefined, and what an "almost unlimited range of subject-matter" may be I have not the slightest idea, though this phrase does seem to rule out chemical equations. Here, then, is one difficulty in my theme. We do not know what we are talking about, except pragmatically.

A second problem follows. The phrase "the Jeffersonian view of man" implies some sort of generalization advanced as truth, but the novel is under no obligation consistently to assert any general truth. It has struggled with general truths many times but the results have not always been happy. In Jefferson's lifetime, for example, Godwin's *Caleb Williams* was supposed to illustrate the general truths of Godwin's own *Principles of Political Justice,* but such readers as that faded story retains get through it very well without knowing anything about philosophical anarchy. Charles Brockden Brown, Godwin's American contemporary, was supposed to demonstrate Godwinian principles in *Alcuin,* printed in 1798. Perhaps he does, since Part One of that book tells us that "men and women are partakers of the same nature. They are rational beings; and, as such, the same principles of truth and equity must be applicable to both." Alas, however, in Part II, we read: "What avails it to be told by any one, that he is an advocate for Liberty? . . . We shall generally find that he intends only freedom to himself, and subjection to all others." This neatly reverses the Godwinianism of Part I. Moreover, the next year, in 1799, Brown published *Ormond.* Boasting of his superiority to all moral codes, Ormond causes the death of the heroine's father, of his mistress, of the titular villain, and almost of the heroine herself. Did Brown write a half-Godwinian novel in 1798, and all of an anti-Godwinian novel in 1799? If the question seems pedantic, the Dos Passos of the *U.S.A.* and the Dos Passos of the *District of Columbia* trilogy are virtually two separate persons.

Working backward, to be sure, scholarship sometimes traces in a novel the influence of some organized set of ideas. In our time, for example, philosophical assumptions about man's happiness in an indifferent universe have helped to produce the fiction of Kafka and Sartre. But do American followers of Kafka and Sartre imitate the fiction or the philosophy? This is not an idle question. As Malraux tells us in his *Museum without Walls,* painters are inspired by paintings, not by theories, and in the same way novelists are inspired by novels. Scholarship may justly argue from the fiction of Dickens, Hardy, and Meredith as it does in the cases of Dreiser and Stephen Crane, that these writers are expounders of general notions—benevolence, pessimism, evolution, physiological chemistry, determinism, and so on, and scholarship is right to say so. But one must distinguish. Dickens did not read Malthus' *Essay on Population,* strike his desk, exclaim, "Go to, now, I will expose this wickedness," and then produce *The Chimes;* as a matter of fact the book jelled when the church bells of Genoa spun his ideas round and round in a whirl of vexation and giddiness, out of which emerged the Shakespearian tag: "We have heard the chimes at midnight, Master Shallow." There is as much melodrama as metaphysics in Hardy, *The Egoist* owes more to the age of Dryden than it does to the age of Darwin, and Dreiser and Crane, if they borrowed a little determinism for their fiction, did not owe their sense of drama to philosophy. We shall make small progress by naïvely inquiring whether American novelists set out to demonstrate the Declaration of Independence, though we may reasonably inquire whether fiction confirms its tenets. Art is insight, not logical positivism. The Dreiser who gave us the determinism of *An American Tragedy* also gave us the mysticism of *The Bulwark*. Philosophy is to be used by the artist, art is not to be fitted into philosophy.

There is a third question. We really have no canon for judging the influence of the novel. We have had, of course, vivid statements. When Lincoln greeted Harriet Beecher Stowe with the remark: "So you're the little woman who wrote the book that made this great war," we do not argue that his military history was wrong, we properly infer that a great politician recognized a great opinion-making force. Because so many commentators have talked about the Leatherstocking Tales as creating an American myth, we assume a myth was created. We know that Tom Sawyer getting his fence whitewashed has passed into folklore and we infer from the prodigious vogue of *Ben Hur* that Protestant Christians thought they might safely combine piety and excitement by following the immortal chariot race. But single instances do not add up to generalizations. If the Leatherstocking Tales created American myth, was *Moby Dick* equally such a creator? It remained for twentieth-century college professors to say so. If thousands of Christians who read *Ben Hur* were edified, were the thousands of readers who have followed the fortunes of Joe Christmas in *Light in August* equally edified? We are assured by critics that this, too, is a tale of the Christ.

We may lazily agree that the American novel has been an influential force. It is only when we try to define the force that we get into trouble. The novel is a popular form—does it have an equally popular effect? Charles Sheldon's *In His Steps* sold hundreds of thousands of copies, but did it perceptibly influence American conduct? *The Scarlet Letter*, we all agree, is a masterpiece, but its active life is mainly in schools and colleges. Does *The Scarlet Letter* develop an American value system as *Ten Nights in a Bar-Room* by Timothy Shay Arthur does not? Or is the question irrelevant? Some great books—*Huckleberry Finn* is an example—have moved from popular reading into academic society; does this mean that the public was instinctively right and the professors merely belated? Or, considering the meanings that have been read into *Huck,* shall one say the public did not know what it was reading until the critics pointed it out? Shall one argue from popular acclaim or from critical approval— from *The Wide, Wide World, Gates Ajar, The Winning of Barbara Worth,* and *The Robe,* or from Henry Adams's *Democracy,* Henry James's *The Ambassadors,* and Henry Miller's *Tropic of Cancer,* to name three dissimilar highbrow successes? What about science fiction, in which Jeffersonian democracy commonly conquers supermen from Venus or aristocratic tyrants from the laboratory? Or detective fiction? The conventions of that universal form require the punishment of the criminal if the penultimate paragraph finds him still alive. Shall we say this points to American respect for order; or, considering the amount of extra-legal violence in mystery stories, shall we infer that American thrillers increase our contempt for the police? Despite admirable studies of American best-sellers and the vogue of certain books and novelists, the sociology of the impact of fiction upon living is virtually an untouched problem, and it may be that an inquiry into Jeffersonianism and the novel is a merely academic exercise—in the wrong sense of academic.

Finally, how is one to deal with this enormous mass of books? I begin by accepting the judgments of literary history, which are probably pragmatical but are not necessarily false. Specialists have sorted out the titles, and one may safely assume in the case of certain large categories of minor fiction that the volumes are very like each other. For example, one does not have to read every historical romance printed between 1880 and 1914 to discover that they run true to type. As for major figures, time, scholarship, and taste discover importances I think we can safely accept; and though revaluation may thrust a neglected Herman Melville forward and reduce a Francis Marion Crawford to secondary importance, the beaten track of historical scholarship is secure enough, if we keep one caution in mind. We may rest content with standard names, but we should be less certain that they express unvarying standard values. We should not forget that *The Scarlet Letter* was once a daring book, that *Huckleberry Finn* was refused shelf space in public libraries, and that the vividness of the confessions of Holden Caulfield does not make *Catcher in the Rye* acceptable to all American school-boards.

iii

This, however, suggests an important truth. Through the nineteenth century and, indeed, beyond, the purpose of the novel in English, at least, has been in most cases explicitly and in other cases implicitly moral. The doctrine was necessitated in the first instance, among other causes, by the desire to gain literary and social standing for an artistic *parvenu*. Though the Puritans did not utterly condemn fiction, they were skittish about it; and the middle class in the eighteenth century and later, taught that fiction is lies, required the ethical assurance of sub-titles like "a tale of truth," an "authentic history," and so on. If this seems naïve, remember that the art for art's sake theory came late, that Poe, who belabored didacticism, nevertheless had, in Mabbott's phrase, a horror of immoral tendencies, that the basic purpose of Henry James even at his most elaborate is the Socratic "Know thyself," and that the sexual theme in contemporary writing is honestly defended as a drive for moral freedom. The appeal to moral purpose runs all the way from *The Power of Sympathy* in the 1790's to *Franny and Zooey* in the 1960's; and though the claim is occasionally specious, it is on the whole genuine and offers a way to determine how far American novelists subscribe to the Jeffersonian view that men are controlled by "that moral sense of right and wrong, which, like the sense of taste and feeling in every man, makes a part of his nature."

One must make another general observation, though it will be instantly denied by practitioners of the art of what is called "the pure novel," and this is that the novel is essentially an expression of social criticism. One can conceivably write sonnets in solitude, construct a theory of the will in a lonely study, pen religious meditations in a cell, and even write plays, though not very good plays, without much reference to the social order—witness Byron's *Manfred*. But the novel, even the novel about a being as solitary as Robinson Crusoe, is a social, even a sociological, exploration. This truth is sometimes dismissed as a platitude and is, moreover, a truth not always popular among critics. Nevertheless, all novels are in some sense novels of manners. Even the Leatherstocking Tales dramatize a conflict of cultures, even *Moby Dick* asserts that a whaling vessel is a social microcosm, even *Lord of the Flies* assumes an adult world against which to rebel, a political order to parody. The fictional hero-villain of contemporary society, if he hates society, is conditioned by the society he hates. The most macabre books by William Faulkner assume an orderly social pattern however decayed—indeed, it is precisely this assumption that gives them both their power and their confusion. Even the most brutal detective stories of Mickey Spillane and Raymond Chandler accept a social code, urban civilization, traffic regulations, and, eventually, the police. Our inquiry is, then, not aesthetic except incidentally, it is philosophical, psychological, and social. It is even a political inquiry, provided one does not misinterpret political as mere partisanship.

CHAPTER III

JEFFERSONIANISM

i

THE second difficulty in this inquiry is created by Jefferson himself, that most elusive of eighteenth-century philosophers. But before turning to it, I put aside one mildly misleading question; what did Jefferson think about the novel? During his lifetime American fiction was in its infancy, and the British novel was still in a stage of artistic development comparable to Italian primitive painting—admirable in intention, sometimes successful in execution, but often naïve in technique. For that matter, Continental fiction was not more advanced.

Jane Austen's *Pride and Prejudice* did not get written until Jefferson was seventy, *Waverley* until he was seventy-one. He could not make up his mind about this literary upstart. In 1818 he advised Nicholas Burwell that the inordinate passion for novels was a great obstacle to good education and that novel-reading infected the mind and created a bloated imagination, a sickly judgment, and a disgust toward the real business of life. Yet in 1787 he had told Peter Carr that the writings of Sterne form the best course of morality ever written, and in 1771 he wrote Robert Skipworth that a little attention to the nature of the human mind evinces that the entertainments of fiction are useful and pleasant. He once bought a set of Sterne and he once commended certain tales by Marmontel, Madame de Genlis and Maria Edgeworth for their morality. If Jefferson is simplicistic in the one-to-one relation between fiction and morality, he represents his generation. Fortunately not what he thought of fiction but what fiction has made of Jefferson is the problem before us.

I must make a second preliminary observation. The novel principally concerns the relations of men and women; the world of Jeffersonian theory is a masculine world. A child of John Locke, Jefferson knew there was something called the passions, including the sexual urge, but his theorizing mostly concerns the conduct of the male animal. This Virginia gentleman was of course courteous to the female sex, this Virginian demographer could theorize about philoprogenitiveness and the peopling of America, but the obsession with copulation evident in the contemporary novel would have mystified the sage of Monticello. For him sexuality was a fact like climate. The romantics were by and by led to promote sexual sensibility into a paramount place in human psychology, but the bill of rights for Jefferson did not include any paragraph on the wrongs of women. He liked women of refinement, he flirted with some of them, he tried to give his daughters an education proper to gentlewomen, he believed in marriage rather than free love, he helped several unfortunate ladies to straighten out their husbands or their finances, and he made the test of barbarism the question whether women were forced to drudge unjustly. In the *Notes on Virginia* he soundly said: "It is civilization alone which replaces women in the enjoyment of their natural equality," but this seems to mean no more than that we should not imitate the Indians and their squaws. For Jefferson, I very much fear that the place of woman was in the home. Certainly he did not want them in public office, and he said so. In trying to ascertain how far American fiction has supported the Jeffersonian theory of human nature, the masculinity of his formulations is a limitation of some consequence.

ii

What is that theory? No question is more difficult. Of all the great eighteenth-century Americans, Franklin not excepted, Jefferson had the largest and most comprehensive mind. He was a man of the Renaissance born into the Age of Reason. Like Goethe, his great contemporary, he lived to be eighty-three, and he was capable of growth and of self-contradiction to the very end. Shall one educe the Jeffersonian theory from his brilliant youth, shaped by the classics, law, politics, and conversation, and culminating in the Declaration of Independence? Or from the mature, the cosmopolitan Jefferson, who experienced the French Revolution and learned to admire polish and to despise kings? Or from the ancient sage engaging John Adams in the most philosophic correspondence in American political history? The genius of Jefferson, subtle and Hellenic as that of Adams was Roman and stoic, was a product of a period that so delighted in general truths, it is often impossible to distinguish Jefferson's personal opinions from those of the Enlightenment. But since Jefferson possibly contributed as much to the Enlightenment as the Enlightenment contributed to Jefferson, perhaps the distinction does not matter.

Let us begin with the Declaration, which, said Jefferson, was only the common sense of the matter. This asserts a theory of human nature. All men are created equal—a phrase that has long troubled the world. Men have unalienable rights. To secure these rights is the function of sound government. Creation implies a Creator, to whom the Declaration appeals. Man is, then, a being socially defined since equality in a vacuum would be meaningless. If the Enlightenment argued about the origin of rights in some state of nature, the problem for Jefferson in the American Revolution, the French Revolution, the Napoleonic world, and the world of the Holy Alliance was not rights in a state of nature but the puzzle of rights in a universe in turmoil.

We note that this theory is poles removed from the subjectivism of European romantics, who tended to dominate Western thought between 1776 and 1830, and also from the psychoanalysts, who sometimes look on man as a helpless atom suspended in his own unconsciousness and seem to interpret society either as a menace or as a boundary to define or endanger the ego and its own.

Jefferson held a contrary opinion. He was not a subjectivist. As he wrote in 1787, "man was destined for society. His morality, therefore, was to be formed to this object. He was endowed with a sense of right and wrong, merely relative to this. This sense is as much a part of his nature, as the sense of hearing, seeing, feeling; it is the true foundation of morality." Reviewing his career he said in 1823: "We believed . . . that man was a rational animal, endowed by nature with rights, and with an innate sense of justice; and that he could be restrained from wrong and protected in right, by moderate powers, confided to persons of his own choice, and held to their duties by dependence on his will." If this seems a political definition of humanity, we shall have to get along with it.

Clearly, three important components of the Jeffersonian view are a moral sense, social duties, and a doctrine of responsible government. The locus of governmental responsibility was for him a life-long concern, for he devoted his great talents to studying, defining, and exercising governmental responsibility and to checking public officials when he thought they were upsetting the balance between government and the governed. "Every man, and every body of men," he wrote in an opinion submitted to Washington in 1793, "possesses the right of self-government. They receive it with their being from the hand of nature. Individuals exercise it by their single will; collections of men by that of their majority; for the law of the majority is the natural law of every society."

But governmental responsibility is only one side of the equation. There cannot be individual rights without individual duties. That there are such individual duties acknowledged by any people not fettered by tyranny Jefferson affirmed. He attributed the acceptance of the American constitution to "the good sense and good disposition of the people," once they came to understand the "incompetence" of the Articles of Confederation. Enable the people to see that it is their interest to preserve peace and order, he wrote Madison in 1787, and they will preserve it. In his first annual message as president he hoped the empty American land would be settled "by the multiplication of men susceptible of happiness, educated in the love of order, habituated to self-government and valuing its blessings above all price."

Evidently for Jefferson individual responsibility toward society was a function of the moral sense or the moral faculty—terms he used interchangeably. This was a power quite as innate and unalienable as were rights. Much scholarship has been expended in hunting down the origins of this idea among the Greeks, the Romans, the Jews, the Italians, the French, and the British, in Epicureanism, stoicism, Christianity, deism, materialism, and utilitarianism. It will suffice for us to note that Jefferson clung to this concept all his life. Man possesses moral autonomy. "The great principles of right and wrong," he said in 1774, "are legible to every reader; to pursue them, requires not the aid of many counsels." The moral faculty was evident even among the savage Indians. It was the cause of man's "feelings or conscience," he said in 1793, and "the moral duties which exist between individual and individual in a state of nature, accompany them into a state of society, and the aggregate of the duties of all the individuals composing the society constitutes the duties of that society towards any other." For proof he appealed "to the true fountain of evidence, the head and heart of every rational and honest man." "It is there that nature has written her moral laws, and where every man may read them for himself."

But what if the moral sense be defective in particular persons? Where the moral sense is wanting, he wrote in 1814, "we endeavor to supply the defect by education, by appeals to reason and calculation, by presenting to one so unhappily conformed, other motives to do good and to eschew evil, such as the love, or the hatred, or the rejection of those among whom he lives and whose society is necessary to his happiness and even existence, by showing that honesty promotes interest; by legal rewards and punishments; and by the prospects of a future state." Men may differ in morality from one social context to another, but nevertheless "the moral instinct . . . is the brightest gem with which the human character is studded, and the want of it . . . more degrading than the most hideous bodily deformities."

Jefferson repudiated the theory that self-regard is a governing motive. We should as a matter of course, he thought, develop self-respect, but mere self-respect is not morality. "I do not believe with the Rochefoucaulds and Montaignes," he told Mann Page in 1795, "that fourteen out of fifteen men are rogues; I believe a great abatement from that proportion may be made in favor of general honesty." General honesty here implies social responsibility. "What a satisfaction have we," he wrote John Dickinson in 1801, "in the contemplation of the benevolent effects of our efforts, compared with those of the leaders on the other side, who . . . have endeavored . . . to persuade us that man cannot be governed but by the rod. . . . I shall have the happiness of living and dying in the contrary hope." "Nature," he elsewhere said, "hath implanted in our breasts a love of others, a sense of duty to them, a moral instinct, in short, which prompts us irresistibly to feel and to succor their distresses." He repudiated the self-regarding doctrines of some French *philosophes,* declaring that "to say that gratitude is never to enter into the motives of national conduct, is to revive a principle which has been buried for centuries."

Jefferson was aware that both morality and altruism differ from place to place and from time to time. This difference he attributed to human adaptability, to what, like Jeremy Bentham, he called utility—that is, to the pressure of environment upon conduct. But environment does not determine conduct. If like Pascal he knew that truth on one side of the Pyrenees may be falsehood on the other, he was no determinist. The relativity of ethical patterns did not shake his faith in a governing ethical principle, and he dismissed any apparent inconsistency by arguing that in a given set of circumstances utility was the test or aim of virtue. For example, Negro slavery arose from no "depravity of the moral sense." Man is everywhere an autonomous moral being. But he is also an imitative animal. Hence the importance of setting him right examples to imitate.

In 1799 Jefferson wrote William Green Munford a letter that expresses the heart of his doctrine: "I am one of those who think well of the human character generally. I consider man as formed for society, and endowed by nature with those dispositions which fit him for society. I believe also, with Condorcet . . . that his mind is perfectible to a degree of which he cannot as yet form any conception. . . . I join you, therefore, in branding as cowardly the idea that the human mind is incapable of further advances. This is precisely the doctrine that the present despots of the earth are inculcating & their friends here re-echoing; & applying especially to religion & politics. . . . But thank heaven the American mind is already too much opened, to listen to these impostures. . . . What is once acquired of real knowledge can never be lost. To preserve the freedom of the human mind then & freedom of the press, every spirit should be ready to devote itself to martyrdom, for as long as we may think as we will, & speak as we think, the condition of man will proceed in improvement."

iii

This paragraph is so manifestly affirmative as to lend color to the charge that Jefferson was an optimist, perhaps even a sentimental optimist. Passing over the question why moderns regard optimism as a defect and pessimism as a virtue, I must point out that a reserved, perhaps even a pessimistic, view of man was more characteristic of the Enlightenment than not. If Jefferson had an affirmative belief in man, he reached it with his eyes open. He lived in an age when in Sydney Smith's judgment it was an awful time to entertain liberal opinions. Jefferson had vainly sought to defend his native state against invasion, and he had lived to see the national capital burned by enemy troops. During his lifetime the British Empire was torn asunder, the French Revolution had followed, the old monarchy went down in a blood bath, Napoleon emerged out of the murk of corruption to convulse the world from Buenos Aires to Moscow, dynasties had risen and fallen, new nations had come into being, and Europe of the Holy Alliance, its thinking shaped by Burke, Friedrich Gentz, de Maistre, Bonald, and Metternich, smeared Tom Paine, vilified Jefferson, sent liberals into exile, produced the nationalism of Fichte, the pessimism of Schopenhauer, and the transcendental determinism of Hegel. It also maintained order by the bayonet from the Argentine to Siberia.

Jefferson was no mere do-gooder. Every government, he said, has in it "some sort of corruption and degeneracy, which cunning will discover, and wickedness insensibly open, cultivate and improve." History, he wrote in 1787, mainly tells us what bad government is. He told Madison ten years later: "in truth I do not recollect in all the animal kingdom a single species but man which is eternally and systematically engaged in the destruction of its own species. What is called civilization seems to have no other effect on him than to teach him to pursue the principle of *bellum omnium in omnia.*" In his *Autobiography*, written at seventy-three, he declared there were three epochs in history signalized by the total extinction of national morality—the age of Alexander, the age following the death of the first Caesar, and his own. Even in the New World, he wrote, Americans "should look forward to a time, and that not a distant one, when a corruption in this . . . country . . . will have seized the head of government, and be spread . . . through the body of the people. . . . Human nature is the same on every side of the Atlantic." It cannot be said of him, as is sometimes said of Emerson, that he ignored evil. The utmost Jefferson could hope was to slow down the inevitable cyclic movement from improvement to decay.

But how? His faith resembles that of Goethe:

> *Ein guter Mensch in seinem dunkeln Drange*
> *Ist sich des rechten Weges wohl bewusst.*

Not by failure of psychological nerve could the strivings of honest men be guided through a dark, tempestuous era toward the good. "I will not believe our labors lost," he wrote Adams in 1821. "I shall not die without a hope that light and liberty are on steady advance." The first need was to get out of Europe and to stay out. Let American travelers view European courts as one would a menagerie "with their lions, tigers, hyenas, and other beasts of prey." The next need was to achieve and maintain simplicity—hence Jefferson's curious notion that farmers were inherently incorruptible. In the third place, set before the rising generation the examples of great and serene individuals, living and dead, and of great systems of thought. In the fourth place, anticipate John Stuart Mill on liberty by allowing differences of opinion "to purify themselves by free discussion" and so leave the horizon "more bright and serene." But above all put your trust in ingenuous youth educated into freedom by schools that ground the rising generation in "the first elements of morality"; and replace the artificial aristocracy of the Old World by a new, natural, and flexible aristocracy of talent in the New. Select regularly "the best geniuses" combed "from the rubbish," since nature has sown talent as liberally among the poor as among the rich. Thus selected, natural leaders in republican virtue, appealing to the good sense of the Americans, will at least long postpone cultural and political decay.

To many modern minds the doctrine and the diction seem alike outmoded. But let us not confuse accidents and substance. Jefferson thought it less important to know that men may reason wrongly than to realize they have the faculty of reason, less important to know there are moral monsters than to comprehend that one cannot measure moral monstrosity unless one first possesses moral standards, less important to dwell upon the defects and possible fate of government than to discover what the essence of government truly is. If Jefferson's world seems obsolescent because his phraseology is not modern, we may modestly remember that our own scientific psychology may also have its little day and cease to be. In construing the eternal struggle between the ego and the id Freud was sufficiently Jeffersonian to prefer rational control to passional anarchy, and as between inner-directed man and other-directed man David Riesman, if I understand him, comes out for moral autonomy. When in our day the president of the Carnegie Foundation gets out a book on the need for excellence in our culture and follows it with another on individualism and the innovative society, it is just possible he is revalidating a Jeffersonian idea. The vocabulary of the founding fathers does not deserve our patronage but our comprehension. We may be Jeffersonians without knowing it.

CHAPTER IV

THE CLASSICAL NOVEL BEFORE JAMES

i

By the classical American novel I mean the kind of novel that writers produced in this country between 1789 and 1917. I call this novel classical in the sense that one calls a symphony classical. A symphony is built upon an intelligible plan common to composer and auditor that yields the auditor an intellectual anticipation of the musical structure and restricts the ground plan of the composition. A symphonic poem is not of this order even when its title—for example, "Til Eulenspiegel's Merry Pranks"—may arouse intellectual anticipation. But the anticipation aroused by a symphonic poem is not the anticipation aroused by a symphony. Aside from a few eccentric narratives like *Moby Dick,* nineteenth-century American novels resemble the symphony rather than the symphonic poem.

Other classifications of fiction are of course possible. One might refer, for example, to the standard novel. But this term implies a kind of literary carpentry, a sort of B-class book, and I want to avoid this imputation. My term also ignores an important distinction in nineteenth-century American fiction between the novel and the romance, a distinction, as Terence Martin has shown, that has both metaphysical and cultural importance, and one of consequence to Hawthorne, Cooper, and James. But for the present purposes we can ignore this difference.

What then do I mean by the classical American novel? The classical novel is a story with a plot. The concept of plot carries with it the as-

25

sumption of a firm intellectual and, as it were, externalized control of narrative, whether the tale be simple or complex. By intellectual externalized structure I mean in the first place structure intelligible as idea, not as caprice, and in the second place structure approaching the conditions of drama as usually defined. This structure will not importantly involve unpredictable associational or irrational psychology as in *The Sound and the Fury,* but will be such that the story line can be summarized without reference to private, symbolical, or subconscious meaning more important than event. *The Scarlet Letter* and *A Hazard of New Fortunes* have this character; *Look Homeward, Angel* does not. You cannot summarize *Look Homeward, Angel* any more than you can summarize a flowing stream.

In the classical American novel structure mounts as in drama through times and passions toward some sort of denouement, climax, resolution, or crucial decision that ends the book. The reader's attention has all along been subtly pointed to this necessary scene, his expectations have been aroused as the narrative moves toward resolution. This climax can be intellectually anticipated before it occurs and intellectually justified after it happens. Thus the confession of Arthur Dimmesdale in *The Scarlet Letter* is anticipated by the reader and is aesthetically justified in retrospect. There is no such scene in *Look Homeward, Angel*; whether such a scene exists in *The Sound and the Fury* is matter of dispute. But the classical novel cannot admit a disputable climax; its resolution must have no effect of being improvised, intruded, or accidental but must be the necessary end to which the whole narrative has tended.

Since resolution implies the ending of conflict, the classical novel chronicles forces in states of increasing opposition leading to climax. In its simplest manifestation (as in melodrama) this conflict is between obviously good persons and obviously bad ones, but in any novel pretending to art the discovery of goodness or badness is artfully delayed. The revelation, however, always comes, and is ultimate. In simplest terms the conflict is between the hero and the villain. Although these words together with "heroine" suffice for *Othello,* our departure from the classical novel is so great that one uses them today almost with apology.

Since we shun writing with too palpable a design upon us, the moral significance of hero, heroine, villain, and any other leading character in the classical novel will be enriched and complicated by any major novelist. Thus Hawthorne, James, and Howells delight in overlaying the simple concepts of heroism or villainy with minute and deceptive touches of the brush beyond the capacity of Cooper and Mark Twain. Nevertheless, the essential polarities remain, and the reader is made to yield his allegiance to the forces of good and to abhor or pity the forces of evil. Thus Gilbert Osmond of *The Portrait of a Lady* is complex, but there is small doubt he is a villain, just as there is small doubt that Isabel Archer, whatever her temperamental complexities, is the suffering heroine. Whether the treatment of episode be scenic or panoramic, whether the book move along the line of time like *The Last of the Mohicans* or play tricks with time as does *A Connecticut Yankee at King Arthur's Court*, whether the tale enforce an ancient ethical truth as does *The Rise of Silas Lapham* or call one into question as does *The Scarlet Letter*, the classical novel by the law of its being incarnates conflicting values in its principal characters and states a moral problem. So fundamental is this necessity that a boy's book like *Tom Sawyer* has a villain named Indian Joe, and as ironic a commentary as *The House of Mirth* has a hero—so weak, it is true, as to be almost imperceptible—named Lawrence Selden.

Characters in the classical novel act from intelligible motives and seek intelligible ends. The skillful novelist will enrich both motive and aim with all kinds of velleities and possible self-deceptions, but the aim and the motive will remain. These novels also accept more formalized description, dialogue, and explanation than is customary in contemporary fiction; and this formality is part of the intellectual appeal of the volume. Such elements rest upon an assumption shared by writer and reader that time and place, thought and communication are parts of an intelligible world-order—a world-order that may be satirized as in Cooper's *The Monikins* and Melville's *Mardi* but that is fundamental to the existence of fiction.

In one respect the analogy of the symphony is misleading. Except as style we are not conscious of the presence of the composer in the musical composition. But in the classical novel the author may be present not only as style but also as commentator and even as intruder. Thus in *The Sea Lions* Cooper interrupts his narrative of life in the Antarctic night to assure us that Samuel F. B. Morse really did invent the telegraph, Hawthorne intrudes into *The Marble Faun* to give us views on the place of women in the social order, and Henry James in *The American* interpolates his opinion of American English spoken in the West. From our point of view a novel is flawed when the author intrudes, but the classical novel makes no such austere demand, and the author may not only explain and comment on character or episode, but also talk generally, as do Cooper and Mark Twain.

ii

When one passes from these general considerations to our first great classical novelist, James Fenimore Cooper, five preliminary matters should be got out of the way. The first is that Cooper is much more than a writer of adventure stories for boys. The second is that Mark Twain's funny essay is a quite inadequate estimate of Cooper's achievement—resembling an account of Shakespeare's technique that confined itself to putting Bohemia on the seacoast, letting Cleopatra play billiards in Alexandria, and having a clock strike three in Caesar's Rome. The third is that Cooper's thirty-two novels are spread over more than a quarter of a century, and vary in tone from the idyll of Natty Bumppo in love, in *The Pathfinder,* to such dark and bitter books as *Wyandotté, Jack Tier,* and *The Ways of the Hour.* The fourth is that Cooper was not merely a social critic of Europe and America, he was a moralist also, and that his ethical principles do not vary from his first novel to his last. The fifth is that there is no childhood in Cooper—no little Pearl, no Huck Finn, no Maisie. His people are apparently born into adulthood, and though they grow old, they were never young.

The obvious fact about Cooper's tales is that they take place in a moral universe. All the vast furniture of heaven and earth, the endless forests, the great prairies, the cities, the limitless expanse of ocean where islands are thrown up as in *The Crater* and ships are wrecked as in *The Pilot*—all this is the creation of a superintending power interested in the moral well-being of man. In Jefferson this power was the God of deism; in Cooper it becomes the trinitarian deity of the Episcopal church. All of Cooper's characters participate in this universal morality.

Except for idiots like Job in *Lionel Lincoln* and the amiable Hetty of *The Deerslayer* Cooper's people are rational beings acting from comprehensible motives for understandable ends. Like Jefferson, Cooper assumes the existence of an innate moral sense. One may act in its light as Leatherstocking does and as Miles Wallingford comes in time to do, one may smother it as do Magua in *The Last of the Mohicans,* Mahtoree in *The Prairie,* and Spike in *Jack Tier,* or one may waver. Thus Ishmael Bush in *The Prairie,* Scalping Peter in *Oak Openings,* and Deacon Pratt in *The Sea Lions,* each long misled, come by and by to have glimpses of the light. Still a fourth group, even though they know better, do not smother the moral sense but disguise it, turn it into self-interest, deny the Jeffersonian premise of altruism, and threaten the rights and the property of others. Such are Jason Newcome in *The Chainbearer,* Steadfast Dodge in *Home as Found,* and Ithuel Bolt in *Wing-and-Wing,* who are not so much villains as rascals upon whom a society cannot be built. In Cooper woman is the purer vessel, possessing a finer instinct for the good, but there are remarkable exceptions to this general rule, like Mrs. Mosely in *Precaution,* Mrs. Lechmere in *Lionel Lincoln,* Mrs. Budd in *Jack Tier,* and Mary Monson in *The Ways of the Hour.* No conclusion can be drawn from the fact that most of these more or less wicked females are middle-aged women who are or who have been married. In his interpretation of the universe and in his acceptance of an innate moral sense Cooper shares Jefferson's theory of existence, which he Christianized; he shares also other Jeffersonian attitudes, such as a distrust of the press, a distrust of cities, and a dislike for the nascent industrial order.

Cooper believed in a republic rather than a democracy; and if he devoted one kind of book—for example, *The Bravo*—to exposing the evils of autocracy, he devoted another kind—for example, *The Crater*—to exposing the weakness of an ochlocracy. Like Jefferson he thought there is a natural aristocracy, but Cooper inclined more to birth and breeding than to native genius. Representatives of this aristocracy, inspired by a sense of public duty, will protect the rights of other men, guide the people wisely if the people will but choose them as leaders, and subordinate their own personal interests to the public good. Opposing like Jefferson a crude laissez-faire philosophy, or the stake-in-society doctrine of selfishness, Cooper leads Sir John Goldencalf in *The Monikins* to accept the view that the stake-in-society doctrine is wrong. Although the responsibility of the elite is for the general good, some gentlemen, of course, never measure up to it—for example, Captain Willoughby in *Wyandotté.* Judge Templeton in *The Pioneers* and Mark Woolston in *The Crater* accept public responsibility but are thwarted by demagogues, and Hugh Littlepage in *The Redskins* is likewise thwarted, but eventually triumphs. Cooper was not a Whig; but neither was he a Jacksonian Democrat.

Cooper apparently does not accept the Jeffersonian distrust of inheritance in land. Some eight of his novels turn upon the inheritance of estates. But if Cooper does not agree that the earth belongs to the living, he does believe that landed estates should be administered for the general good in a society that, like it or not, will for him forever fall into ranks and classes.

In general Cooper, then, accepts and enforces a Jeffersonian theory of human nature. A disturbing doubt arises in Cooper as he grows older and confronts an increasing moral ambiguity in American society. Men, he thought, can be taught or encouraged to exercise a self-control for the good of others, but his later fictions express a growing sense of the weakening of morality in American life. The problem over which he came to brood concerns not so much the moral sense, the existence of which he does not deny, but the proper application of it, the possible refusal of moral leadership by a vulgar and materialistic nation.

Nevertheless Cooper's world is still the world of Thomas Jefferson. In a solid and three-dimensional universe operated by a benevolent deity, human beings act from cognizable motives; if they are virtuous they subdue their passions to reason; and they are conscious of the need to follow the Jeffersonian principle of altruism—rascals and villains alone act from self-interest. The moral sense is of course sometimes disguised as the Christian conscience, but the Christian conscience is here simply a more advanced stage of the moral sense, although there are many passages— indeed, whole books—by Cooper that can be interpreted to mean that the people are a great beast. Cooper's novels, despite their Hamiltonian flavor, are operative in a Jeffersonian world.

iii

In the fiction of Hawthorne the substantial universe of Cooper dissolves until we scarcely know whether we live in past or present time— in a world as solid as the Great Stone Face or one as dreamlike as fancy's show-box. In his case, too, certain preliminary considerations should be stated. Of the thirteen volumes Hawthorne published in his life five do not concern us, nor do the fragments of fiction that appeared after his death. The early *Fanshawe* can be dismissed, but the three collections of tales and sketches, more uneven in quality than scholarship allows, are useful as corroboration for values in the four major novels. We may set aside Hawthorne's predilection for Gothic romance that so queerly obfuscates the plots of *The Blithedale Romance* and *The Marble Faun,* and we should be careful not to be overly bemused by Hawthorne's interest in the New England past nor by contemporary analyses that turn everything in Hawthorne into a symbol for something else. Finally I suggest that if Hawthorne's Christianity lacks the firmness of Cooper's Episcopalianism, words like "soul," "dream," "spiritual," and "the ideal" are operative terms in his work. I have no sooner said this, however, than I realize there are two Hawthornes (there are as a matter of fact a great many!)—the Hawthorne who liked tobacco-chewing mountaineers, Irish emigrants, tavern keepers, farmers, politicians, and vagabonds; and the Hawthorne who felt that "the ideal" in the transcendental sense, though humanly unattainable, was, nevertheless, just around the corner, that the unpardonable sin was possible to a select few, that town pumps could write, fauns turn into human beings, portraits control the living, and mirrors reflect the images of the dead.

To Hawthorne the paramount sin lies not in sensuality but in intellectual arrogance that not only seeks to transcend mortality but, perverting the natural affections, destroys the autonomy of others. This is the sin of Ethan Brand, of Dr. Rappacini, of Aylmer in "The Birthmark," of Wakefield, who out of vanity stayed away from his wife for twenty years, of Clifford Pyncheon, who, released from prison, thinks the world owes him happiness, of Zenobia in *The Blithedale Romance,* who tries to absorb the life of her unacknowledged sister into her own, of Miriam in *The Marble Faun,* who, aware of Donatello's simplicity, uses that simplicity to commit murder, and of Chillingworth in *The Scarlet Letter.* In that astonishing masterpiece the wronged husband becomes the villain because he manipulates the supposedly affectionate relation developed between himself and the minister, to torture Dimmesdale, drive him to confession, and then to his death. In comparison with this egotism Hester Prynne is justified in saying earlier to her lover: What we did had a consecration of its own. Their sin was not, in this sense, one against man.

Egotism not merely perverts the moral sense, it also violates the natural order. As Hawthorne writes in one place: "Amid the seeming confusion of our mysterious world, individuals are so nicely adjusted to a system, and systems to one another and to a whole, that, by stepping aside for a moment, a man exposes himself to the fearful risk of losing his place forever." "No sagacious man," he makes Coverdale declare in *The Blithedale Romance,* "will long retain his sagacity, if he live exclusively among reformers and progressive people, without periodically returning into the settled system of things, to correct himself by a new observation from the old standpoint." There is here, certainly, something of Calvinism, something of the doctrine of the fortunate fall, as a passage at the end of "Fancy's Show-Box" indicates: "Man must not disclaim his brotherhood, even with the guiltiest, since, though his hand be clean, his heart has surely been polluted by the flitting phantoms of iniquity." So, too, at the conclusion of *The Marble Faun* Kenyon, the *raisonneur,* says it is too late in the world's history for creatures like Donatello, who live only for happiness; they must change their natures or else perish like the antediluvian creatures before us. But all this does not mean that change is forever impossible.

Like Jefferson, Hawthorne finds the dead hand of the past unbearable —indeed, his preoccupation with New England partly arises from his desire to expose that life for the evil thing it was. The Jefferson who thought the earth belongs to the living, who destroyed a royal government, primogeniture, and an established church, who wanted to destroy slavery, and who declared he was the enemy of every form of tyranny over the mind of man would have applauded Holgrave's powerful speech in *The House of Seven Gables*: "A dead man sits on all our judgment seats. . . . We read in dead men's books! We laugh at dead men's jokes, and cry at dead men's pathos! We are sick of dead men's diseases . . . and die of the same remedies with which dead doctors killed their patients! . . . Whatever we seek to do, of our own free motion, a dead man's icy hand obstructs us! . . . If each generation were allowed and expected to build its own houses, that single change, comparatively unimportant in itself, would imply almost every reform which society is now suffering for. I doubt whether even our public edifices . . . ought to be built of such permanent materials as stone or brick. It were better that they should crumble to ruin once in twenty years . . . as a hint to the people to examine into and reform the institutions which they symbolize." Lest we might still miss the point, Hawthorne flatly declares in the preface that he has written the novel to show how "the wrong-doing of one generation lives into the successive ones, and, divesting itself of every temporary advantage, becomes a pure and uncontrollable mischief," and he hopes the book may convince mankind "of the folly of tumbling down an avalanche of ill-gotten gold, or real-estate, on the heads of an unfortunate posterity to maim and crush them." The same denunciation of the dead past appears in *The Marble Faun* where it is proposed that all towns should be made capable of purification by fire, or of decay, within each half-century, and where Kenyon tells Donatello that, whatever the faults of young America, in Italy it seems "as if all the weary and dreary Past were piled upon the back of the Present." The two are then symbolically surrounded by a swarm of beggars. Returning to *The House of the Seven Gables* for a moment, I note with amusement that Hawthorne includes among the *dramatis personae* a scanty flock of degenerate chickens who, on being transported elsewhere, recover their natural health. If there is in Hawthorne a dark streak of fatalism, he is no determinist.

But in one respect this novelist outstrips Cooper and anticipates a philosophy of motivation that will end by destroying the Jeffersonian system. Hawthorne discovers what we would today call depth psychology, a psychology of repression and occasional escape, of the fashionable modern doctrine of *Angst*. "There is evil," he wrote in his notebooks, "in every human heart, which may remain latent, perhaps, through the whole of life." This he repeats in a story called, significantly, "The Haunted Mind." "In the depths of every heart there is a tomb and a dungeon, though the lights, the music, and revelry may cause us to forget their existence, and the buried one, or prisoners, whom they hide." But the prisoners often escape—for example, in "Fancy's Show-Box," "The Wedding Knell," "The Minister's Black Veil," "Young Goodman Brown," and "The Birthmark." We read in "The Birthmark": "The mind is in a sad state when sleep, the all-involving, cannot confine her spectres within the dim region of her sway, but suffers them to break forth, affrighting this actual life with secrets that perchance belong to the deeper one." And this consciousness of powerful irrational forces in the heart conditions much in the novels; for example in *The Marble Faun,* where Miriam, in a discussion of the myth of Curtius, who leaped into a chasm to preserve Rome, says: "The firmest substance of human happiness is but a thin crust spread over it (i.e., the pit of blackness), with just enough reality to bear up the illusory scenery amid which we tread. It needs no earthquake to open the chasm." Hilda, in reply, would bridge the chasm with good thoughts and deeds; but if, as many critics suspect, the hidden crime in Miriam's past is incest, the figure is significant. One notes with a shudder that she encounters her persecutor in the catacomb of St. Calixtus. Gothicism is here re-enforced by a foretaste of Freud.

But if the solid world of Cooper dissolves in the atmospheric effects, now light, now dark, of Hawthorne, there is nothing in Hawthorne's life, despite his distrust of democracy, and little in his fiction, despite his subjectivism and his symbolism, that makes him antithetic to the Jeffersonian postulates. Characters in Hawthorne do not vote or participate in specific public issues as the characters in *The Monikins* and the Anti-Rent trilogy discuss public policy, but this is less because Hawthorne feels these matters are minor than because for his purposes they are centrifugal. There is town government in *The Scarlet Letter,* there are provincial administrations in the short stories, Judge Pyncheon is, after all, a public official, and *The Blithedale Romance* pictures an orderly society in which everybody obeys regulations that are self-imposed. Man in Hawthorne has a moral sense, perhaps even an oppressive moral sense, and he is, however faintly, a rational being. The basis of the republic may not be as clear in Hawthorne as it is in Cooper, but it is nevertheless there, and Hawthorne does not despair of the republic.

CHAPTER V

JAMES, HOWELLS, MARK TWAIN

i

INASMUCH as my inquiry concerns rationality and moral values rather than beauty or art, the problem of the antebellum novel in the South, the question of its absolute worth being waived, is here relevant. But it is a minor problem. This fiction is politically and socially conscious to a high degree. From John Pendleton Kennedy through William Gilmore Simms the Southern novel was usually engaged in defending or explicating a social and political pattern satisfactory to slave-holders, so that, despite the intrusion of too much blood and thunder into a book like *Nick of the Woods* by Robert Mongomery Bird, and of turgid sentimentality into Mary Jane Holmes's *Tempest and Sunshine* (the authoress, it is true, was born in Massachusetts), no category of American letters is more self-consciously political.

Obviously the Southern novel was explicitly or implicitly anti-egalitarian, and to this degree anti-Jeffersonian. But one must here distinguish between the novel of political apology and the novel of civic responsibility, between the anti-egalitarianism of the Greek democracy Parrington defined as the South Carolina ideal, and the assumption that all men, including faithful slaves, are dowered at birth with an instinctual moral sense and some capacity to reason. Southern theorists sometimes ignored Jefferson and Southern propagandists sometimes turned fiercely against him, but Southern heroes and heroines are capable of rational choice, a feeling for the good, and a proper sense of the place of emotion

35

in human life. The same is true of the slave, who, when he is treated humorously, becomes the theme of comedy not because he lacks the endowments of the white man but because he may have them in a lower form and express himself in an inferior way. But the loyalty of the slave to his master springs from ethical instinct, just as the responsibility of the master for the welfare of the slave in these books springs from a moral faculty educated by Christianity. The settlement, the frontier post, and the plantation in this literature occasion responsible and reflective leadership; typical are the actions of the disguised Lord Craven in Simms' *The Yemassee*. The basis of this whole library is laid in the eighteenth century—in the intellectual milieu out of which Jeffersonianism came; and if the stories are overlaid with romantic colorings borrowed from Scott, Bulwer, Byron, and Tom Moore, be it remembered that Sir Walter's values were shaped by the Scottish Common Sense philosophy, Bulwer in a novel like *Paul Clifford* propounded that anti-romantic doctrine, utilitarianism,* Byron advised everybody to return to Pope, and Moore's satires, like the *Epistles, Odes, and Other Poems* (1806) occasioned by his American tour, are half in the manner of Pope and half in the manner of the Regency. There are, of course, villains in this Southern library—Indians, Negroes, whites—and these villains have perverted their innate moral faculties and reason fallaciously. But this is not anti-Jeffersonian. Except in the matter of human equality, none of this fiction denies the Jeffersonian view of man as a being endowed with reason and with a moral sense. Furthermore, the structure of antebellum Southern fiction is the structure of the classical novel. Nobody imitates Sterne except incidentally; nobody anticipates the novel as flow (as in the case of Thomas Wolfe), nor the novel as a problem of time, consciousness, and decay (as in the case of *The Sound and the Fury*), nor the novel as an exposure of the false doctrine that man's reason is his most human characteristic (as *The Tropic of Capricorn* exposes this doctrine). One may add that Jefferson himself had doubts as to whether the Negro was not biologically inferior to the white man, so that even the fact that the antebellum novel reduced the Negro to inferior status does not totally contradict Jefferson. It merely supports one of Jefferson's doubts.

More troubling than the antebellum Southern novel is the puzzle of Herman Melville. This puzzle has several components; and its solution is not helped by the enthusiasm of Melville specialists, who are often

---

* The one famous sentence in *Paul Clifford* runs to the effect that the worst use you can put a man to is to hang him.

something less than critical where their idol is concerned. In the first place most of Melville's books are not novels in the sense I am using the term "classical novel." *Typee* and *Omoo* are autobiographical adventure stories. *Mardi* is not a novel in any usual sense. *Redburn* and *White-Jacket* are half-confessional (as George Borrow is half-confessional) and half-fictional, but the fictional pattern is not that of the classical novel. *Moby Dick* is *sui generis,* a compound of adventure, philosophy, metaphysical speculation, and probing into human nature. *Pierre* is, in the words of a handbook of American literature, more carefully plotted than written, and I for one would deprecate making it a central book in any interpretation of Melville's general views or his artistic achievement, though the structure is more nearly classical (in my sense) than is the structure of *Redburn. Israel Potter* is of course a sound historical romance. The one book, aside from *Moby Dick,* that takes us straight into the heart of Melville's ethical position is the admirable *Billy Budd,* but *Billy Budd* was not published until 1924 when Melville had been dead for thirty-three years. One cannot, confronted with this cumbrous splendor, neatly split off Melville the novelist from the rest of Melville, so that the problem is complex.

What is equally perplexing is the question: which Melville is one talking about—the nineteenth-century Melville, or the Melville who is the construction of twentieth-century criticism? In the nineteenth century, it is notorious, Melville was the man who lived among the cannibals; and while it is not wholly true that nineteenth-century readers did not think of him as a novelist, it is nevertheless true that they tended to think of him as a writer like Richard Henry Dana, the author of *Two Years Before the Mast,* that admirable combination of an adventure yarn and social criticism. Some nineteenth-century readers apparently also wanted to force *Moby Dick* into this category, into which *Typee* and *Omoo* admirably fit. Melville's interpretation of human nature in *Moby Dick* and *Billy Budd* (one ought perhaps to include *Mardi*) is basically anti-Jeffersonian so far as rationality as a commanding motive is concerned, and may be anti-Jeffersonian so far as the moral sense is concerned. But is *Billy Budd* pro or anti the moral sense? Critics debate endlessly. It can be argued that the ethical basis of *Billy Budd* is egalitarianism, and that part of the theme of *Moby Dick* lies in the tension between a human being of commanding power and doubtful ethics, and a crew of understandably simple ethics and less commanding power. I cannot solve the puzzle, but I suggest that the vogue of Melville is a twentieth-century vogue and that, as our present concern is with the American novel in the last half of the nineteenth century, all that one can do here is to note the dilemma and pass on.

Let us pass on to an artist often considered the greatest American novelist—to Henry James. What of Jeffersonianism amid the intricate patterns of James, who began writing just as Hawthorne died? Since the Jeffersonian theory is conceived in universals, it should not matter that James's fascination with Europe, his eventual end as a British subject, are antithetical to Jefferson. Unlike Howells, James is no egalitarian; and furthermore, his American travel books have an anthropological air as of a cultivated explorer reporting on the naïve customs of rude, colonial tribes. It is, however, true that in the confrontation of Europe and America James finds many Americans, however simple, morally superior to corrupt European families like the Bellegardes in *The American*. Against this truth one must set his passionate admiration for the British upper class with their country houses, their infinite leisure, their taste, and their courtesy. Nevertheless, the Jamesian universe would, one suspects, have bewildered and possibly antagonized that American country gentleman, Thomas Jefferson. It is a world without labor, without industry, without commerce, without religion, and without political responsibility. In *The Princess Casamassima*, the solitary excursion into the lives of the proletariat among the major novels, the little radical group around Hyacinth Robinson is viewed from the outside, and Nicholas Dormer in *The Tragic Muse*, as soon as he is elected to parliament, resigns his seat to pursue art—no doubt, an admirable endorsement of inner integrity, but an act of civic irresponsibility that, if it were generalized, would destroy government.

The benevolent deity of Jefferson disappears. From his Swedenborgian father and from his buoyant philosopher brother, the novelist took over a vague cosmic hope, but his basic stoicism is radically different from the Epicureanism of Jefferson. This stoicism is best expressed in a letter to Grace Norton in 1883: "I don't know *why* we live—the gift of life comes to us from I don't know what source or for what purpose; but I believe we can go on living for the reason that (always up to a certain point) life is the most valuable thing we know anything about, and it is therefore presumptively a great mistake to surrender it while there is any yet left in the cup. . . . don't, I beseech you, *generalize* too much in these sympathies and tendernesses—remember that every life is a special problem which is not yours but another's, and content yourself with the terrible algebra of your own. Don't melt too much into the universe, but be solid and dense and fixed as you can."

The letter goes on to say that we unconsciously help each other, but the statement, noble in itself, is far removed from the pursuit of happiness as understood by the Jeffersonians, and though the emphasis upon individualism squares with the atomistic psychology of Locke, it lacks, it seems to me, any sense of society, any notion of the individual as citizen.

James's world is of course an upper-class world of personal relations—marriage, divorce, inheritance, parents and children, master and servant. He prefers to cherish the past, as is evident in *The Spoils of Poynton*, not dump it as Hawthorne dreams of doing. If an ambiguity of evil bathes his world, evident in *The Turn of the Screw*, the problem of egotism in James is far more complex than it is in Hawthorne. In *The Ambassadors* we are to admire the famous remark of Strether: "Live all you can; it's a mistake not to," but poor Roderick Hudson, given an opportunity to live all he can, goes to pieces. Isabel Archer and Milly Theale follow the law of their being and morally triumph; Daisy Miller and the governess in *The Turn of the Screw* follow the law of *their* being and do not. And what shall one say of that ambiguous person, Christina Light? Or, for that matter, of Caspar Goodwood in *The Portrait of a Lady*, who has all the American virtues? The commands of the moral faculty, if there be one, seem to be as enigmatic as the Greek oracles; and though the central doctrine in James is what an excellent critic has called the ordeal of consciousness, or, if one prefers, the education of sensibility, the clarity of Jefferson's ethics is certainly clouded over in James.

One fact, however, is clear. Although James left to Balzac, Howells, and Zola a moral examination of the means by which money is acquired, he followed his beloved Turgenief in confining his attention to what happens to wealth after it has ripened and mellowed, or as it is lost, or when it has to be striven for if the seeker is to survive in James's novels at all. It is impossible to live in that universe without the possession of money. The need of money drives the Bellegardes to accept Christopher Newman as a prospective son-in-law, the gift of wealth enables Isabel Archer to make her fatal choice among three suitors, the possession of wealth permits Rowland Mallet to bring Roderick Hudson to Europe and disaster. It cannot be said of James that his hero is the five-franc piece, but it can be said that the use of wealth as a basis for morality and culture is his central theme. In him, however, the problem of the proper use of wealth is always personal and inward-looking; it is never a public responsibility.

Another general truth is that James, like Hawthorne, profoundly believes in the autonomy of the individual. No human being can use another human being for self-regarding ends—the sin committed by Gilbert Osmond and Madame Merle, by Kate Croy and Merton Densher. A strong, educated sensibility will deny that self-regarding ends are the goal of life—and James's doctrine is here consonant with Jefferson's repudiation of the self-interest theory of motivation, which is for James the beast in the jungle. The difficulty is that James is by no means sure how the ordinary mean, sensual man is to be lifted to this higher plane of vision and insight. He seems to appeal to general culture, to an aesthetic found mainly among the aristocracy, but even this is not wholly clear. The upper class, for instance, subjects Maisie to a very curious course in self-education in *What Maisie Knew*, and no amount of culture will make Gilbert Osmond anything but a cad. In *The Golden Bowl* Maggie Verver presumably has a great moral triumph, especially a triumph over "the horror of finding evil seated all at its ease where she had only dreamed of good," but the nature of her victory is more than a little puzzling, since Charlotte and the Prince continue to accept at its face value the canon of living in which they grew up. Somewhere in *The Awkward Age* a character is made to exclaim: "Let us not, for God's sake, be vulgar— we haven't yet, sad as it is, come to that"; and though we cannot charge James with the ideas of his characters, I find it a little difficult to know whether he is opposing evil or vulgarity or both. Is a sin against taste also a sin against the holy ghost? No such ambiguity arises in Hawthorne.

One may get as many interpretations of this great novelist as one desires to collect, and I cannot claim special insight, but it would appear that Jeffersonianism in James diminishes to two principles, which as I state them sound flat enough but which, in their working out, James makes exciting. The first is his undoubted sense that there is evil in the world and his undoubted belief that specific evils can always be courageously faced and sometimes overcome. The second is his reverence for the human personality, even when it is as mean as that of Gilbert Osmond, for whom, even, James insists, there is something to be said. If the Jeffersonian state could not quite be erected upon the novels of Henry James, his heroes and heroines and sometimes his victims have an inner integrity and, on occasion, a Christlike capacity for sacrifice that the sage of Monticello would, I think, understand and approve.

iii

The friend of such opposed personalities as Henry James and Mark Twain, William Dean Howells returned to America from Venice just as James began serious writing, and in 1872 published his first novel, not much more than a travel sketch, called *Their Wedding Journey*. Except for *A Foregone Conclusion* (1875), his work is negligible until at the age of forty-five he brought out *A Modern Instance*, a book beginning a series extending to *The Son of Royal Langbrith* (1904) that, as Everett Carter says, is a kind of continuous narrative of American life. Howells early showed his mastery of the psychology of middle-class wives and daughters and his command of American conversational idiom, interests that have but a tangential relation to the essential masculinity of the Jeffersonian theory.

There is of course a current misconception of Howells as a superficial and timid writer who confined himself to the more smiling aspect of life as the more American. This unfortunate phrase appears in *Criticism and Fiction* (1891), and three revisions of the paragraph have not sufficed to kill the error of interpreters. Howells did not say *he* was confining himself to the more smiling aspects of life, but that in comparison with the French and with *Crime and Punishment* American novelists were doing so because conditions in the New World were an improvement over those in the Old. It should, however, cheer those who equate literary success with pessimism to know that Howells goes on to declare that American novelists have only a feeble grasp on urbane life, that conditions in the United States are steadily worsening, and that even in America "where the race has gained a height never reached before, the eminence enables more men than ever . . . to see how even here vast masses of men are sunk in misery that must grow every day more hopeless, or embroiled in a struggle for mere life that must end in enslaving and imbruting them."

Like Hawthorne, Howells was handicapped by the literary conditions of his time. Part of this problem had to do with the prudery of magazine editors and part of it lay in the fact that, in H. H. Boyesen's famous figure, the American girl, supposed to be shy, like an iron virgin crushed every writer into sentimental conformity with false romanticism, false sentimentalism. Deeper, of course, lay Howells' distrust of the passions —a distrust that links him with Jefferson. Modern criticism has no patience with this attitude, which it equates with mock modesty. But the credulity of passional scenes lies forever in the mind of the reader. For me the struggle of Lady Glencora in Trollope's *Can You Forgive Her?* to overcome her obsessive love for Burgo Fitzgerald is far more moving than the sleeping-bag scenes in *For Whom the Bell Tolls,* just as Marcia Gaylord's obsession for Bartley Hubbard in *A Modern Instance* is more poignant than the love affair of Catherine Barkley and Frederick Henry in *A Farewell to Arms.* But these are private judgments.

Howells took a Jeffersonian view of reason and the passions. "If a novel flatters the passions," he wrote, "and exalts them above the principles, it is poisonous." For him the passions were more than the sexuality to which we have reduced these dark powers—they included pride, possession, greed, and self-will, and he thought that a man dominated by his passions and stripped of his reason was only an animal. This is obviously straight Jeffersonianism, supported by Howells' Swedenborgian belief in a moral governor of the universe, in the existence of conscience as an intuitive moral guide, in social obligations, and in an egalitarianism originating in the democracy of the Middle West he knew as a child and reenforced by his reading of Goldoni, Tolstoy, Gronlund, and others. As he told the guests at his seventy-fifth birthday dinner: "For equality, which is justice writ large, is now the hope of humanity; and its service is the condition which has effected itself even in the mystical source where the inspirations of art have their rise." I am not sure I understand this, but it seems to mean that the novelist must be a democrat. For Howells as for Jefferson and William James the universe is fundamentally moral. Novelists who think they are realists because they look on brute passionality as the basic force in human conduct do civilization, so Howells thinks, a profound disservice.

The mind of Howells was an eighteenth-century mind projected into the later nineteenth century, a mind that took instinctive pleasure in lucidity, in eccentrics, and in eccentric speech as Addison, Steele, Fielding, and Goldsmith did, a mind like theirs, that attacked on sight every manifestation of snobbery, the target of Howells' displeasure from his first novel to his last. For Howells as for these eighteenth-century men, all are alike the children of God. Howells' mind was a mind long sealed by Swedenborgianism, by the *Atlantic Monthly,* by Brahmin Boston, by its own astonishing success, against the brutalities of the Civil War and the Gilded Age, and the harsh conflict between capital and labor that raged from at least 1877 until Howells' death in 1920.

But it was also a mind capable of awakening to what Howells in a typical phrase called an emotioning in the direction of the humaner economics. A consciousness of harsh injustice came alive with the Haymarket riot of 1889. One year earlier Howells had published *The Rise of Silas Lapham,* his masterpiece in the old vein of personal morality. *The Rise of Silas Lapham* is a perfect example of the law of *hubris,* for Silas is the architect of his own disaster. The skillful revelation of his psychology, together with that of his notable wife, make this novel one of the finest technical achievements in nineteenth-century fiction. But Howells had learned that the ethical mis-adventures of a New England tycoon were not the total American story. In 1889 he wrote *Annie Kilburn*; in 1890, *A Hazard of New Fortunes*; in 1894, *A Traveler from Altruria*; in 1897, *The Landlord of Lion's Head*; in 1904, *The Son of Royal Langbrith,* all studies in entrepreneurial enterprise in which the novelist comes to grips with the responsibilities of wealth, station, or culture for the welfare of man.

"If America means anything at all," says Mr. Twelvemough in *A Traveler from Altruria,* "it means the honor of work and the recognition of personal worth everywhere." Before we dismiss this as a platitude let us remember the structured society of Cleveland and McKinley. No book by Howells has been more persistently misread and no book by Howells more clearly shows his radical Jeffersonianism. Both here and in its sequel, *Through the Eye of the Needle* (1907), Howells is humorous but merciless in judging contemporary America by the Jeffersonian code. Call it admiration for Tolstoy, call it Christian Socialism, call it the influence of Edward Bellamy or of Gronlund, the attitude is that of a convinced egalitarian who believes that the moral sense is present in every adult. No other nineteenth-century American novelist is so evidently and so profoundly of the Jeffersonian philosophy.

iv

But what about Howells' great friend, Mark Twain? Twain is not so much a novelist as he is a primary force, like the Mississippi River: a collection of his posthumous work is rightly entitled *Mark Twain in Eruption.* He tries everything—public lectures, travel books, historical romance, fantasy, children's stories, scatological masterpieces, science fiction, philosophy—in an effort to express his rich, tormented, and extraordinary personality. He is at once Aristophanes and La Rochefoucauld, Goldsmith and Jonathan Swift. Of twenty major titles published in his life only eight, if one classifies the Joan of Arc book as history, are in any sense fiction; and of these one is written with a collaborator, two are children's books, *The Connecticut Yankee* is fantasy, no one claims distinction for *The American Claimant,* the powerful *Puddin'head Wilson* has *Those Extraordinary Twins* attached to it like a parasitical fungus, and *The Man That Corrupted Hadleyburg* is an eighteenth-century *conte.* The incomparable *Huckleberry Finn* remains, a masterpiece of the first order, but a masterpiece the secret of which, if one takes the critics seriously, nobody knows. If *The Gilded Age* and *Puddin'head Wilson* are indictments, *Huckleberry Finn* is an earthly panorama that must be matched with the panorama of heaven in *Captain Stormfield, Letters from the Earth,* and *The Mysterious Stranger.*

Was Twain a Jeffersonian? One remembers Bernard De Voto's sage observation that Twain can be found on both sides of any question. A common humanity unites Huck and Jim, Roxana and Puddin'head Wilson, Hank Morgan and the serfs whose lot he tries to better, Tom Canty the pauper and little Edward the prince. Surely this wide humanity ranks Twain with Jefferson. Laughter, moreover, is a democratic solvent. No other American has more mercilessly pilloried sham, hypocrisy, and the exploitation of man by man, no other has attacked cruelty more fiercely. But neither the spirit of Swift nor that of Aristophanes necessarily makes one a democrat; and for one apparent reason and two substantial causes one finds that Twain turned away from the Jeffersonian theory of man.

The apparent reason is political, but not the political reason that immediately comes to mind. Twain's disgust with public venality was more immediate than that of Howells, as is evident in *The Gilded Age* and in other works. Indeed, it is difficult to find in him any sympathetic handling of the American political process. My doubts arise, however, from Twain's profound and growing distrust of the populace and from his belief that rule must be imposed from above. Let anyone read the passage in which Colonel Sherburn in *Huckleberry Finn* castigates the mob, note the contempt for humanity in *The Man That Corrupted Hadleyburg,* discover that Tom Sawyer's village is ruled by the elite, find that Hank Morgan the Connecticut Yankee is an enlightened despot with a turn for mechanics, and follow Twain's uncritical admiration of Slade the reformed road-agent, for the all-powerful Mississippi river pilot, for Napoleon III, Cecil Rhodes, General Grant, Henry H. Rogers, and British colonial rulers, and he will discover this truth. This is not, of course, the whole of Twain's politics. He became a mugwump, he denounced King Leopold, he decried much in the missionary movement, but he also liked power, glamor, men who got things done, an attitude that moves him uncomfortably close to Carlyle and Kipling, both of whom he admired, and away from Thomas Jefferson. One cannot forget that his most characteristic phrase about humanity is "the damned human race," and the damned human race must, he thought, be governed by the wise and the powerful.

All this may be disputed, but on two other counts the facts are clear. Twain launched the most scathing attack upon the moral sense in all American literary history, and he was in deadly earnest in doing so. Here is a characteristic passage from a posthumously published essay on "The Damned Human Race": Man, he wrote, "is constitutionally incapable of approaching [loftiness of character]" for he is "constitutionally afflicted with a Defect which must make such approach forever impossible, for it is manifest that this defect is permanent in him . . . I find this Defect to be *the Moral Sense* . . . It is the secret of his degradation. It is the quality *which enables him to do wrong.* It has no other office. It is incapable of performing any other function. . . . Without it, man could do no wrong. He would rise at once to the level of the Higher Animals. . . . What . . . do we find the Primal Curse to have been? Plainly what it was in the beginning: the infliction upon man of the Moral Sense; the ability to distinguish good from evil, and with it, necessarily, the ability to *do* evil; for there can be no evil act without the presence of consciousness of it in the doer of it. And so I find that we have descended and degenerated, from . . . some microscopic atom wandering at its pleasure between the mighty horizons of a drop of water . . . insect by insect, animal by animal, reptile by reptile, down the long highway of smirchless innocence, till we have reached the bottom stage of development—namable as the Human Being." And, as he says in *Letters from the Earth,* the church is utterly wrong in saying the Moral Sense sets man above the animals; on the contrary, it sets him below the beast, for "he is always foul-minded and guilty, and the beast always clean-minded and innocent." This is "like valuing a watch that must go wrong, above a watch that can't."

In such a creature the pursuit of happiness is a contradiction in terms. Satan tells the boys in *The Mysterious Stranger*: "Are you so unobservant as not to have found out that sanity and happiness are an impossible combination? No sane man can be happy, for to him life is real, and he sees what a fearful thing it is. Only the mad can be happy, and not many of these." Twain denies *in toto* the pursuit of happiness, the concept of altruism, the notion of rationality as a controlling force, and the doctrine of republican virtue.

The second incontrovertible reason for placing Twain among the anti-Jeffersonians is that, reverting to an ancient theory repudiated by Jefferson, he was a determinist to whom man was a machine not controlled by itself. This idea he picked up in the fifties, he made it the subject of an address to the Monday Evening Club in Hartford in 1883, he re-worked his statement of it during his second residence in Vienna, and he published it privately in 1906 as *What Is Man?* Doubtless *What Is Man?* is naïve as metaphysics, but its viewpoint was sincerely held. As he told Albert Bigelow Paine: "When the first living atom found itself afloat on the great Laurentian sea the first act of the first atom led to the second act of that first atom, and so on down through the succeeding ages of all life, until, if the steps could be traced, it would be shown that the first act of that first atom led inevitably to the act of my standing here in my dressing-gown at this instant talking to you." He wrote Twichell, having read Jonathan Edwards on *The Freedom of the Will*: "I think that when he concedes the autocratic dominion of Motive and Necessity he grants a third position of mine—that a man's mind is a mere machine—an *automatic* machine—which is handled entirely from the *outside,* the man himself furnishing it absolutely nothing." The supremacy of self-interest in Twain couples with a doctrine of the impossibility of moral autonomy. Every man's temperament, he thought, was elected for him in the first instant of creation, and he believed also that no change of government, no alteration of moral ideals could effect the total sum of human misery: "From everlasting to everlasting this is the law: the sum of wrong & misery shall always keep exact step with the sum of human blessedness. No civilization, no advance has ever modified these proportions by even the shadow of a shade, nor ever can, while our race endures." Twain once described man as a "basket of pestilent corruption provided for the support and entertainment of swarming armies of bacilli—armies commissioned to rot him and destroy him . . . The process of waylaying him, persecuting him, rotting him, killing him, begins with his first breath, and there is no mercy, no pity, no truce till he draws his last one."

Huck Finn may feel sorry for the King and the Duke, tarred and feathered and ridden on a rail; Mark Twain may denounce Belgian and American imperialism; an ineffectual and corrupt republican government may even be better than the government of the czar; pity and sympathy are preferable to brutality; but it is all one for Twain: "We describe a man by his vicious traits and condemn him, or by his fine traits and gifts, and praise him and accord him high merit for their possession. It is comical. He did not invent these things; he did not stock himself with them. God conferred them upon him in the first instant of creation. They constitute the law, and he could not escape obedience to the decree." For Mark Twain the universe might be intelligible but it was humanly meaningless, and it was to this predicament that he who was perhaps the most powerful prose master of the American nineteenth century brought the Jeffersonian doctrine when he died in 1910. The doctrine of life, liberty, and the pursuit of happiness as attainable ends came in the hands of the greatest American humorist to be that set forth in a quatrain of the *Rubáiyat*:

> With Earth's first Clay They did the Last Man knead,
> And there of the Last Harvest sow'd the Seed;
>   And the first Morning of Creation wrote
> What the Last Dawn of Reckoning shall read.

CHAPTER VI

YESTERDAY AND TODAY

i

IN some sense the half-century from 1870 to 1920 was the golden age of the American novel. Not only was the period illustrated by mature work by James, Howells, and Mark Twain, the half-century was rich in lesser talents and productive of important variations on the form. The talented include such writers as Francis Marion Crawford, Jack London, Albion W. Tourgee, Booth Tarkington, Paul Leicester Ford, S. Weir Mitchell, Thomas Nelson Page, Henry Blake Fuller, Harold Frederic, Frank Norris, and Hamlin Garland, each in his way "dated," yet each an intelligent craftsman to whose ability reigning schools of scholarship and criticism are less than just. On the whole these writers and their contemporaries were content with the formula of the classical novel, and on the whole the public, whether the general public (whatever that means) or the elite group of the "literary," were also content. There were mutterings about too much morality, too many happy endings, and too much avoidance of raw life, but it would be difficult to say that the mutterings were essentially different from the discontent of Poe's generation with the literary life of his time.

The period is notable among American literary epochs for its interest in, its devotion to, craftsmanship as a corrective to the sentimental and romantic indiscipline that had preceded it. Craftsmanship was made a central consideration by a variety of interests, among which three are of considerable consequence. One was the habit of serializing fiction in literary magazines here or in Great Britain and the Empire, a practice that demanded special attention to plot and structure—the same kind of attention one finds in Dickens, Thackeray, Trollope, and Wilkie Collins. Another was that a leading "note" in literary criticism, exemplified in the essays of J. Brander Matthews, was a revival of Poe's dedication of criticism to craftsmanship. Matthews (and others) insisted that the architecture of a novel is as essential to its value as construction is to a play, and he thought that the business of the critic was to master the secrets of craftsmanship, convey them to the reader, and judge the book as much in the light of its formal excellence as in the light of its philosophy or its aesthetic appeal. A third was the increasing interchange of imaginative works and criticism between Great Britain and the United States during a period when the craft of writing was also a paramount issue in Great Britain. The vogue of Stevenson, Kipling, A. Conan Doyle, Stanley Weyman, and other practitioners of the well-made novel was as great in the United States as it was in the British Empire.

Finally, it is to be noted that the moral issue was likewise vigorously discussed. It was the epoch of the so-called problem novel, as in the instances of *The Damnation of Theron Ware, The Open Question, Tess of the D'Urbervilles,* and *The Woman Who Did,* just as it was the age of *A Doll's House, Ghosts, The Second Mrs. Tanqueray, Mrs. Dane's Defence, Sapho,* and *Bought and Paid For* on the stage; but the problem novel, though it called conventional judgments into question, never called the possession of the moral sense into question, and both criticism and fiction were so intent upon rationality that many plays and some novels read for whole pages as if they were transcripts of a debating society. Shaw is of course the shining instance. In *Mrs. Warren's Profession* that lady argues more earnestly for righteousness than does the clergyman in Howells' *The Minister's Charge.*

There were, of course, other movements. The decadence, aestheticism, and the art-for-art's-sake cults scarcely disturbed the surface of American fiction, though somebody is ever and again rediscovering the plush fiction of Edgar Saltus. Naturalism, if novelists had consistently followed its doctrine, would have destroyed Jeffersonian psychology and Jeffersonian civic responsibility. But American fictionists seldom stuck to the terrible logic of the naturalist doctrine as Mark Twain did in *What Is Man?,* and their struggles to be terrifying remind one of the Fat Boy in *Pickwick Papers,* just as their struggles to be metaphysical remind one of the clergyman in Boswell's *Johnson* who informed the Great Cham that he was trying to be philosophical but somehow, he knew not why, he always found cheerfulness breaking in. Bitter Bierce was a consistent determinist, but he wrote no novels, unless one wants to linger on that pastiche, *The Monk and the Hangman's Daughter.* Stephen Crane's *Maggie* is claimed for naturalism, perhaps rightly, but to me it reads like melodrama with overtones of stagey humor. In *The Red Badge of Courage* a sense of shame (and that, after all, is instinctive morality) drives Henry Fleming back to his regimental duties. One has to turn to Crane's shorter tales like *The Open Boat* and *The Monster* for more consistent naturalism. Norris's *McTeague* is more deterministic than *The Octopus,* but Norris is clearly on the side of rational order in the first book and clearly of a reforming mind in the second and in its sequel, *The Pit,* in which not merely cheerfulness but sentimentality breaks in. Garland is a reformer; and Jack London wavers between the attractive moral righteousness of the animal kingdom (*The Call of the Wild*) and the attractive moral perfection of utopian socialism. Dreiser is a more complex case. He talks about "chemisms" as determining conduct, and no continuing state could be founded on *Sister Carrie,* I suppose. But social justice triumphs (as does moral justice) in *An American Tragedy,* Frank Cowperwood's career is in some sense the career of a paper dragon, and Dreiser moved in the direction of socialism, of communism, and eventually of moral mysticism in *The Bulwark.* Before World War I naturalism as doctrine may have threatened the Jeffersonian interpretation but did not dethrone it.

Nor, with all its emphasis upon environmental conditioning, did the local-color movement alter anything. Local colorists preferred the short story, but local-color novels abound—Tarkington's *The Gentleman from Indiana,* Westcott's *David Harum,* Eggleston's *The Hoosier Schoolmaster,* Ed Howe's *The Story of a Country Town* are, at varying levels, typical books. Some of these works—for instance, *The Story of a Country Town* —perhaps question seriously the Jeffersonian theory, but on the whole the local-color writers seldom threaten its presuppositions. The characteristic defect of the movement was sentimentality, its characteristic solution of the problem of evil is an appeal to the better nature of the culprit or the villain, the characteristic point of the novel is plain good sense, the shrewdness and kindliness of the average American.

An enormous number of novels during this half-century were novels of political exposé or of political reform. *The Gilded Age* is a plea for honest government, Winston Churchill's *Coniston* and *Mr. Crewe's Career* expose the hold of the railroads on New Hampshire, Paul Leicester Ford's *The Honorable Peter Stirling,* based on the career of Grover Cleveland, like *Mr. Deeds Goes to Washington,* encourages the seeker to go bravely on, novels by Brand Whitlock, David Graham Phillips, Robert Herrick, and Albion W. Tourgee want to improve political life north or south, Edward Bellamy in *Looking Backward* looks forward, and writers of such diverse personal philosophies as William Allen White, Ellen Glasgow, Upton Sinclair, and Robert Grant try their hands at fiction that prophesies or mirrors various progressive movements culminating in Woodrow Wilson's *The New Freedom*. Almost invariably these books want to turn back to the simplicities of the Jeffersonian world. Almost invariably the hero is a young lawyer of a Lincolnian cast of mind who, slowly awakening to civic indignation, ferrets out the skulduggery, appeals in plain words to the plain people, and, authorized by their electing him to office, turns the rascals out, the rascals being politicians and malefactors of great wealth and their hypocritical clerical apologists. This fiction seems faded today, but it was devoted to the proposition that you can't fool all of the people all of the time, and was a viable literary form as late as Sinclair Lewis's *It Can't Happen Here* (1936).

ii

One cannot consider everything, but I must linger for a moment with three women novelists of aristocratic temperament and refined sensibility —Edith Wharton, Willa Cather, and Ellen Glasgow—who, better than any other writers, bridge the gap between the novelists I have just been discussing and the revolution in fiction that came about after 1920. Each condemned the materialistic society of her time, each looked backward to a happier era, and each found flaws in that earlier age. Thus Edith Wharton knows that little old New York was stuffy, Willa Cather, if she gives us in Ántonia Shimerda the healthy woman of the frontier, also gives us Marian Forrester of *A Lost Lady*, whose career is downward, and Ellen Glasgow's portraits of helpless Southern females like Virginia in the novel of that name and Mrs. Birdsong in *The Sheltered Life* are an indictment of sentimentalism as an evil force.

Nevertheless, other leading personages created by these writers are motivated by rationally understandable desires and sustained by an ethical will of the kind Jefferson had in mind. Or, if they fail to follow a proper moral imperative, the reader is made to comprehend their folly and to understand the false reasoning (or sentimentality, or egotism) that led them into it. Thus in *The House of Mirth* Lily Bart is as she is because of nature and nurture, but she rises to the moral height of Christopher Newman in *The American* when she refuses to revenge herself upon the group that has degraded her. So in *Barren Ground,* by Ellen Glasgow, Dorinda Oakley not only learns to live wisely without joy but goes to the length of taking in and mothering the man who had betrayed her. The simple goodness of Ántonia in *My Ántonia* fills the whole book with joy, *The Professor's House* is a study in contrasts between simple, fundamental morality and sham altruism, and *Death Comes for the Archbishop* shows that man can be man in the Jeffersonian sense even among the crudities of the frontier.

These are representative novelists of the transition, whose books could be paralleled by the achievements of others—for example, Robert Herrick. Their general faith in something like the Jeffersonian interpretation is the more remarkable because as the nineteenth century melted into the twentieth, two great intellectual shifts were in progress that powerfully affected the fictional acceptance of democratic man. The first change, which reaches back into the eighteenth century, is the substitution of a dynamic for a mechanical concept of the universe and of human life. In its earlier aspect this shift usefully denied what Oliver Wendell Holmes called mechanism in thought and morals, and, even if the universe grew somber, assured the novelist (as in the case of these three writers) that man was in some degree master of his fate and captain of his soul. In its later phase the shift masquerades under the varying interpretations one associates with Marx, Darwin, Spencer, Freud, and Watson. In this second phase the faculty psychology weakened or disappeared along with the vanishing of the Scottish Common Sense school as the quasi-official philosophy of American academic institutions. The intellectual and cultural environment, therefore, of the later novels of Mrs. Wharton, Miss Glasgow, and Miss Cather was dark, and their sense of the heroism of living one's life on an acceptable ethical plane was at once increased and made more difficult. Miss Glasgow began as a Darwinian (or Spencerian) naturalist in a book like *Phases of an Inferior Planet* but she ended in the Sophoclean serenity of *Vein of Iron* and *In This Our Life.* Presumably the crucial date in this intellectual history is the publication by William James in 1890 of his *Principles of Psychology,* a book in which James denied that the concept of the soul was a useful psychological idea. There is little about the soul in Miss Glasgow, who was steeped in Darwin, Spencer, and, by and by, James, but she clung to heroism, to the tacit heroism of lonely individuals who will not surrender either their reason or their moral choice.

But these writers, like most of those discussed in the earlier part of this chapter, are out of fashion. They lack vogue largely because of a crucial change in the assumptions of American fiction, a change taking place between 1920 and 1945. This change has not only affected the notion of the novel as an autonomous literary form, it has radically altered the concept of the novel as a responsible work of art in a democracy struggling to achieve its ideals in a world that seems leagued against the existence of the democratic republic in the Jeffersonian sense. It is, therefore, important to inquire what contemporary fiction reveals about belief in modern man living in a democratic state. Inasmuch as the novel was characterized by Stendhal, a writer much admired by the moderns, as a mirror moving down the road, and by Henry James, whom they also admire, as a large, lucid reflector, it seems proper to ask what the mirror and what the reflector, or rather what the images from the mirror and reflector as recorded by novelists, have to tell about the presence or absence of Jeffersonian theory.

iii

Undeniably American fiction since 1920 has entered into a new and important phase, one that has powerfully aided in making American writing one of the major literatures of the contemporary world. Not since the generation of Howells, James, and Mark Twain have we had a like galaxy of important novelists, some of whose books will certainly endure. The technical proficiency of this fiction is often high. Compare, if you please, any first-rate mystery story with, say, Anna Katharine Green's *The Leavenworth Case* of 1878 at one level or, at another, *The Sound and the Fury* as a Southern novel with the *Red Rock* (1898) of Thomas Nelson

Page, and the advance is dazzling. Some of the major character creations of recent and contemporary fiction are surely memorable—Fitzgerald's Gatsby, the major personages in Faulkner's better books, the "hero" in *Catcher in the Rye*. Whatever one thinks of its art, *Ship of Fools* has a spread of canvas not often found in American fiction. The movement has produced stylists of great purity like Jean Stafford and rhetoricians of great, if uneven, power like Thomas Wolfe. It is important enough to be powerfully attacked by moralists and powerfully defended by sympathizers.

But contemporary taste does not always produce lasting aesthetic judgments. For example, Sir Walter Scott was often brigaded with Shakespeare by nineteenth-century critics (and still is by Scottish writers), but with us he has mainly sunk to the level of a school classic dutifully read (or unread). There was little doubt a hundred years ago that Bulwer was a great genius; who reads Bulwer nowadays? The enthusiasms of any aesthetic system are the enthusiasms of that aesthetic system, and beyond this quiet historical truth we cannot go. I propose, therefore, to waive all questions of the imaginative power (which is often great), of the beauty (which is sometimes notable), and of the probable lasting value of this fictional library, and address myself to its substance rather than to its art, more particularly, to those elements that illumine what its creators accept or fail to accept of the Jeffersonian theory of man as a human being living in political society. What do the moving mirror and the lucid reflector reveal about life in the beleaguered American republic of the mid-twentieth century?

Well, of the Jeffersonian premises the first one that has evidently disappeared in the body of modern fiction approved by criticism as serious art is any belief in providence, in an all-wise deity, in a rational universe, and in any human capacity to understand that universe, whether it be rational or not.

My second observation is that man as citizen has virtually vanished from this fiction; or, if and when he appears, it is either as a vicious demagogue or as a witless voter. John Dos Passos, it is true, was later to return nostalgically upon Jeffersonianism, but a representative democracy is impossible in a country like that pictured in *Manhattan Transfer* and the three novels that make up *U.S.A.*, books devoted to lives that are aimless, greedy, rootless, and for the most part without moral scruples. In the fiction of Robert Penn Warren organizations simple and democratic in their beginnings are driven to violence and murder, as is true of the tobacco farmers in *Night Rider*, and the career of Willie Stark in *All the King's Men* is a case of a democrat evolving into a demagogue.

The political control of Yoknapatawpha County, studied in Faulkner's trilogy, *The Hamlet, The Town,* and *The Mansion,* lies in the hands of the Snopes family. These representative Americans are listed in a recent issue of the *Book-of-the-Month Club News* as: Ab Snopes, founder, horse thief and barn-burner; Flem Snopes, the shrewdest and most avaricious of them all; Byron Snopes, bank clerk and bank robber; Clarence E. Snopes, a state senator well-known to brothel-keepers in Memphis; Doris Snopes, blessed with the mentality of a child and the moral principles of a wolverine; Ike Snopes, an idiot; I. O. Snopes, a bigamist, swindler and schoolmaster; Mink Snopes, a murderer; Montgomery Ward Snopes, a purveyor of pornography; Orestes Snopes, a thwarted murderer; Wesley Snopes, a singing teacher run out of town on a rail; and four nameless Snopes children who once cooked and ate a pedigreed Pekinese. There are two others, Eck and W. P. Snopes, who are honest and industrious but who are therefore suspected of not being true members of the family. Against these one will of course want to project the figures of V. K. Ratcliff and Gavin Stevens, the latter of whom translates the Old Testament into Greek, of both of whom it is fair to say that like the Celts they always went forth to battle and they always fell.

Most Americans live in cities. What is city life like? The lives of businessmen as pictured by John O'Hara, Nathanael West, and Budd Schulberg are empty. The irresponsible heroes of Sherwood Anderson always walk away. Life in Chicago as portrayed in the Studs Lonigan trilogy of James T. Farrell and in subsequent volumes is unattractive, and so are the skid row in Nelson Algren's *The Man with the Golden Arm* and *A Walk on the Wild Side,* the Negro ghetto of Richard Wright's *Native Son,* the slums of Willard Motley's *Knock on Any Door,* and the alternate orgiastic sexuality and tedium of Henry Miller's *Tropic of Capricorn,* subtitled "On the Ovarian Trolley." Somewhere in *The Adventures of Augie March* that hero observes: "There haven't been civilizations without cities, but what about cities without civilizations?"

But what voters are left in the villages and in the countryside? Reports on suburbia and exurbia are not encouraging. As for the village, there are the tangle of frustrated lives in *Winesburg, Ohio,* and *Peyton Place,* the animal-like beings of Erskine Caldwell, the Bundrens and their kind in the novels of William Faulkner, the Joad family and their innocent compeers in John Steinbeck's books, and the curious highway amorality that lends pungency to James M. Cain's *The Postman Always Rings Twice.* The result of the survey invalidates the thesis of a general distribution of either intelligence or the moral sense.

Women gained the voted in 1920. What is their function in this strange society? Women scarcely exist as persons but only as sexual objects moving in space. For example, the three leading heroines in Hemingway's novels —Lady Brett Ashley, Catherine Barkley, and Maria in *For Whom the Bell Tolls*—though they quiver with erotic sensibility, show no trace of general thought. No woman in any novel by F. Scott Fitzgerald has any civic consciousness, though some of them have been graduated from expensive schools. With few exceptions—one is the seventy-year-old Eunice Habersham of *Intruder in the Dust* and one is the aged Dilsey of *The Sound and the Fury*—women in Faulkner's world are, so to speak, bounded by the two polarities of Temple Drake in *Sanctuary* and Mrs. Jason Compton, who whines her way through *The Sound and the Fury*. As a kind of middle point one can select pregnant young girls like Lena Grove in *Light in August*. The theme of Mary McCarthy's *The Group* is scarcely the superiority of the college-educated, and a popular middle-brow book like Irving Wallace's *The Chapman Report* is read not for its sociology but for its sex. When in *East of Eden* Steinbeck wrote: "The church and the whorehouse arrived in the Far West simultaneously" and then proceeded to concentrate on the whorehouse, he summarized a trend somewhat different from that represented by the League of Women Voters.

Where are the voters of tomorrow supposed to come from? Are they to be like Holden Caulfield of *Catcher in the Rye*, to whom the entire adult world is (in his own language) phony, or like Saul Bellow's Augie March, whose adventures are usually on the shady side of the law, or like Joel Knox in *Other Voices, Other Rooms*, whose move into the adult world is described by one critic as "a straight-line development from the outside world of Moon City through the decadent limbo of Skully's Landing to the private, dreamlike ruins of the Cloud Hotel"? Or like William March's *The Bad Seed*, which restores the Calvinist view of children but subtracts Calvinism? Is the effect of higher education represented by a novel like *The Optimist* of Herbert Gold? Of these books it can be said that they are concerned with everything about the American college except instruction. Finally, the Nick Adams stories of Hemingway's *In Our Time* and the story of Isaac McCaslin in Faulkner's "The Bear" are commonly interpreted as narratives of initiation, but nothing in either author, whatever his excellences, indicates any feeling that a young American should be initiated into a world of political responsibility.

If one asks how order is maintained in the America of these novels, one will learn from a body of detective fiction, some of it brilliantly written, that the police are almost invariably so stupid that they cannot solve a crime, which must be done for them by a sharp-witted private eye, himself often given to violence; and that when the cops are not engaged in arresting the wrong man, they spend a great deal of their energy clubbing prisoners or riding down strikers as in the radical novels of the thirties surveyed by Walter B. Rideout. As for the rural constabulary, here is how a group of South Carolina village policemen, justly arresting Eugene Gant and his friends for drunken driving, are pictured by Thomas Wolfe:

> Their faces had a look of a slow and powerful energy, a fathomless and mindless animal good nature, and at the same time a fathomless and mindless animal cruelty—instant, volcanic, and murderous— written terribly somehow into their wide, thin and horribly cruel mouths, in which there was legible a vitality that had all the wild and sensual force of nature packed into it, and was therefore beyond nature—almost super-natural—in its savage and mindless qualities.

All that these storm-troopers do, however, is to lock up the boys until somebody appears and pays their fines. In view of the brutality of the segregation troubles in Mississippi, this may seem prophetic but it was written in 1935 and concerns an event, real or imaginary, occurring some fifteen or twenty years earlier; and, in any event, showers on village policemen an excessive amount of the supernatural.

The republic has to be defended against its enemies, as even the pacific Jefferson knew. War is dirty business, as Ambrose Bierce and Stephen Crane had already informed American readers. How was the war to make the world safe for democracy regarded? Novels of merit about World War I were written by Thomas Boyd, E. E. Cummings, John Dos Passos, William Faulkner, Ernest Hemingway, and William March, author of *Company K*. Among the more celebrated passages in this library is one in *A Farewell to Arms*: "I was always embarrassed by the words sacred, glorious, and sacrifice and the expression in vain. . . . I had seen nothing sacred, and the things that were glorious had no glory, and the sacrifices were like the stockyards at Chicago if nothing was done with the meat except to bury it." For this reason Frederick Henry makes a separate peace—that is, he deserts, as John Andrews also does in *Three Soldiers*. "I was not made to think," says Frederick Henry simply. War is made, Passini, one of the ambulance men, remarks, because "there are people who are afraid of their officers." One may have every sympathy with this interpretation and yet find it difficult to know how the armed forces of the republic are to be maintained without duty, a word that, though it is not on Henry's list, is apparently among the embarrassing terms that lack the grave quality of place names. These alone possess dignity, according to Hemingway.

In the fictional treatment of World War II there are two separate streams. One, represented by Hersey's *A Bell for Adano,* which ventures to picture the American officer as rather a decent sort, is condemned by many critics as sentimental. The other, represented by Norman Mailer's *The Naked and the Dead,* receives much critical applause. In this book there is no representative of humanely educated intelligence except Lieutenant Hearn, who is treacherously sacrificed by the hard-boiled Sergeant Croft. There is of course General Cummings, a proto-fascist, who thinks the war will release the potential of America and transform it into kinetic energy, and who tells Hearn that in politics, "the trick is to make yourself an instrument of your own policy. Whether you like it or not, that's the highest effectiveness man has achieved." Hearn does not like this, nor would Jefferson. The privates in the military unit on the island of Anapopei display an amazing endurance, cunning, courage, and group loyalty, but their allegiance is mainly to Sergeant Croft, the flashbacks of their lives nowhere display any civic sense, though they are soldiers of the republic, their language, exceedingly rich, is scarcely literate, and the principal motive power of their lives outside the army is an indiscriminating sexuality. It has been argued that the heroes of fiction arising out of World War II realize that indifference and timidity have made them guilty of and responsible for the fact of war and they earn their individuality by relinquishing it. Perhaps. A historian would find it difficult to comprehend how a modern republic can survive if it must depend upon the vulgar intelligence of the soldiers pictured in *The Naked and the Dead* and James Jones's *From Here to Eternity.*

What is even more instructive not only about leading novelists between 1920 and 1945 but about novelists approved by critics since that era is that goodness in America always lies in the past, as with Faulkner, or is a mirage on the horizon as in Saul Bellow's *Herzog* (1964), in which technique takes the place of substance as a central figure teeters on the verge of insanity for 341 pages.

Jefferson had said in his First Inaugural: ". . . too high-minded to endure the degradations of others; possessing a chosen country . . . ; entertaining a due sense of our equal right to the use of our own faculties, to the acquisitions of our own industry, to honor and confidence from our fellow-citizens . . . ; enlightened by a benign religion . . . inculcating honesty, truth, temperance, gratitude, and the love of man, acknowledging and adoring an overruling Providence, which by all its dispensations proves that it delights in the happiness of man here and his great happiness hereafter . . . what more is necessary to make us happy and prosperous people?" The one thing more was, he thought, a wise and frugal government which shall restrain men from injuring one another. Hemingway, perhaps, in *For Whom the Bell Tolls,* John Dos Passos in his later phase, notably in his book on Jefferson, one or two others—for instance, Allen Drury in *Advise and Consent*—respond to this forward-looking theory, but the American novel as approved by critics is filled with gloom, with guilt, with alienation, with *Angst,* with frustration. This interpretation scarcely cheers those who hailed the publication of *The Papers of Thomas Jefferson,* launched in 1950, as a significant historic event.

It may be argued that I cite only one sort of novel, omitting works by writers from Robert Nathan to Conrad Richter less gruesome, less pessimistic, or less violent in character. Among critics, middle-brow novelists like Herman Wouk, Gerald Warner Brace, Sloan Wilson, and Edwin O'Connor are treated as popularizers unworthy of serious aesthetic analysis. Moreover, if one consults the reading lists for college courses in recent fiction, one will seldom find *The Man in the Gray Flannel Suit* but one will almost invariably find writers like Norman Mailer, Saul Bellow, and Nathanael West. Among standard critical interpretations of fictional trends, leading volumes have such significant titles as *The Novel of Violence in America, New American Gothic, The Dungeon of the Heart,* and *The Power of Blackness.* Ours is, I think, the only period in the history of the American novel in which it has been possible for a learned German to publish a monograph on erotic scenes in American fiction.

If little serious academic criticism has been lavished upon *Advise and Consent,* a novel which insists that when the chips are down even in the American senate most men act morally, Mr. Joseph J. Waldmeir, writing in *The Nation* in 1961, informs us that since man must either compromise with or conform to society, or be destroyed by society, novelists avoid the dilemma by creating a third choice: disaffiliation both from society and from crusades against social evils. Society, he says, is deterministic, but he argues that the individual, particularly the novelist, is somehow free to conceive society as being completely determined, yet somehow containing a small group of individuals who retain freedom and avoid determinism. If they were born free, why were not the others? What is meant by compromise? What is meant by destruction? What is meant by freedom? Man is a political animal, as even Robinson Crusoe knew; and on the basis of whimsical withdrawal from society, if one supposes this to be possible, one cannot maintain the democratic republic which permits novelists the freedom to write against freedom, and Mr. Waldmeir the freedom to say there is no freedom except when novelists declare they are free.

This doctrine of alienation has its farthest reaches, I suppose, in the dedication of Allen Ginsberg's *Howl,* a poem eagerly defended by many critics and scholars. The dedication is to "Jack Kerouac, new Buddha of American prose, who spit forth intelligence into eleven books," to William Seward Burroughs, "author of *Naked Lunch,* an endless novel which will drive everybody mad," and to Neal Cassady, "author of . . . an autobiography (1949) which enlightened Buddha," whatever that means. "All these books," the dedication continues, "are published in Heaven." This neatly avoids the gross competition of the market place, but Mr. Ginsberg fails to give us the mailing address of the firm.

But the wheel has since come full circle. Mr. Saul Bellow, who also believes that the author is alienated from society, nevertheless writes in *The Saturday Review* for April 3, 1965, that most current fiction, apparently not published in Heaven, is "weak, poor, and boring," affirms that the rebellion of nihilism is "grimy and gritty and very boring too," and says it is evident that "polymorphous sexuality and vehement declarations of alienation are not going to produce great works of art." The novelist, he concludes, "must begin to think, and to think not merely of his own narrower interests and needs."

Precisely. This is what Jefferson also thought.

CHAPTER VII

CONCLUSION IN WHICH, PERHAPS, NOTHING IS CONCLUDED

i

THIS analysis has concerned novels that are much in the critical eye. Other types of novels are continually being published and read in the United States—local-color stories, humorous books, tales of adventure, middle-brow novels, detective stories, science fiction, and much else. Many of these display a somewhat more affirmative attitude towards human life and modern culture than appears in the books I have analyzed. I have spoken of Allen Drury's *Advise and Consent*. But a novel like *To Kill A Mockingbird,* a study like James Gould Cozzens' *The Last Adam,* works like Edwin O'Connor's *The Last Hurrah* and *The Edge of Sadness* are of this other sort. They are the kind of book that is widely read by readers seeking intelligent entertainment, they are adopted by book clubs, and they abound in the public libraries. They are, I fear, "wholesome," and they do not commonly figure in contemporary criticism, and are not usually analyzed or set forth as models of composition in the creative writing courses that abound in our colleges and universities. Yet the craftsmanship of fiction like this is, presumably, at least as good as the craftsmanship of James Jones, Saul Bellow, or Henry Miller.

If one assumes that a novel may be quiet and good, if one assumes that a new *Pride and Prejudice, Middlemarch, The Egoist,* or *The Old Wives Tale* were written tomorrow, it would, I suggest, have some difficulty in making its way through the jungle of modern book advertising. I quote

from the *New York Times Book Review* of May 9, 1965, phrases culled
at random from the advertisements of novels, most of which will not live
three months:

> *Gothic mystery, savage modern satire—bizarre, farcical, obscene,*
> *   recondite, but always vividly pictured*
> *Spellbinding novel . . . thrilling, action-charged tale of relentless*
> *   war against the underworld*
> *wicked and hilarious goings-on*
> *electric suspense inside an atomic research laboratory*
> *powerful and shocking*
> *deep and bitter seer, superb romantic poet*
> *an ex-gambler, ex-dope runner, ex-extortionist—son of a*
> *   Protestant minister*
> *slightly demonic, with some evil surprises*
> *Orwellian novel . . . about a youth drug, the men and*
> *   women who peddle this stimulant to increased sexual*
> *   power . . . convincing and appalling.*

There is nothing unusual about this advertising. One can duplicate it
every week. But how maintain a Jeffersonian democracy on wicked and
hilarious goings-on, electric suspense, stimulants to increased sexual
power, convincing and appalling? Or, if this question is too naïve, how
maintain a Jeffersonian society in which language of this sort concerning
the great art of literature, language that is deliberately intended to drug
the judgment and appeal to the sense of excitement only, is standard
language publicizing a branch of the fine arts? Paintings are not thus
publicized nor is music. Advertising has of course always been absurd;
but the vocabulary in which the hucksters sell the printed word passes
beyond absurdity into a kind of Hitlerian madness. We are removed, to
put it mildly, from the world of Howells and Henry James, Hawthorne
and Fenimore Cooper. What causes have thus profoundly altered the
features of the American muse?

ii

One may tentatively conclude that both on the high-brow level and on the level of the ordinary manufacture and sale of fiction the American novel has on the whole ceased to interest itself in the Jeffersonian theory of a presiding deity, human rationality, altruism as a governing motive (one must here except dramatic or melodramatic cases of self-sacrifice), and civic responsibility as marks of maturity. It is possible to enumerate some of the more powerful components of the literary revolution we have experienced.

In the first place American writers have became fascinated by such Europeans as Dostoevski, Kierkegaard, Kafka, Sartre, and Joyce—a writer who began with sensitive narratives, passed into the subconscious, and ended with the nightmare life of H. C. Earwicker, a book so ingeniously technical that only specialists can read it. The Americans, however, seem not to have acquired the profound Christianity that gives meaning to Dostoevski and Kierkegaard and are incapable of the astringent metaphysical logic of Kafka and Sartre.

In the second place the impact of T. S. Eliot, an expatriate American, and D. H. Lawrence, an expatriate Englishman, has been immense. I insist on their expatriate quality not as derogation but as definition, for I think these critics helped to make rootlessness a fashionable theme.

Third, after the publication of John Macy's *The Spirit of American Literature* in 1918 and Lawrence's *Studies in Classic American Literature* in 1923 the criterion of literary success, past or present, became Dionysiac rather than Apollonian. Nietzsche drove out Goethe. The importance of the New England classics save in the cases of Hawthorne and Thoreau came to an end, and the genteel tradition, even when represented by so good a book as Brownell's *American Prose Masters,* was discarded. The rediscovery of Herman Melville after 1920 was an important side effect of this movement. Melville fitted but imperfectly into the pattern of the classic novel and was perhaps not a novelist but the writer of a vast romantic confession couched in symbolism and running to fourteen volumes. In the new interpretation Captain Ahab ceased to be a rhetorical sea-captain who had read too much Byron for his own good, and turned into the incarnation of suffering humanity; and the white whale, no longer a sailor's legend, after a little semantic puzzlement about colors, became the symbol of the blackness of evil in a Manichean universe from which Christianity had disappeared. As for writers like Emerson and Whittier, they were nowhere at all.

In the fourth place there was the enormous vogue of Freud and Jung who, so to speak, for this purpose, became American citizens. The influence of irrational and subconscious psychology on American writing has been partially traced by Frederick Hoffman in his study, *Freudianism and the Literary Mind*. Under that influence and under the influence of a new psychological and psychiatric criticism that sheltered itself under the Freudian umbrella new canons of style and achievement developed. Not what an author plainly says is the criterion of meaning, but what his unconscious dictates to him as metaphor, myth, or symbol opaque to the general reader but transparent to the alert critic. One passed from Joseph Warren Beach's book, *American Fiction, 1920–1940,* a rational examination of prose narrative, to a study like Mr. Leslie A. Fiedler's *Love and Death in the American Novel* (1960), concerning which a historian of American criticism writes: "The archetypal pattern isolated by Fiedler is not one of rebirth but rather of frustration and perversion resulting from the denial of mature sexuality in American literature, a reflection of the psyche of American society. The Oedipal situation supplies the basis for cultural analysis."

Precisely what is meant by "mature sexuality in American literature" I do not know, but that an Oedipal situation is a sound basis for cultural analysis I rather doubt, if by cultural analysis one means the total spectrum of American culture from science to frivolity; and since no qualification of the word is given, I assume that is what is intended. Is our interest in hospitals, astronomy, and symphony orchestras a reflection of the damaged psyche of American society? Do perplexing problems like technological unemployment, desegregation, the apathy of voters, and the annual threat of strikes that will shut down the automobile industry somehow arise from an Oedipal complex? How does the Lever Brothers building in New York reflect a denial of mature sexuality among architects, and in what sense do the paintings of Donald Stoltenberg, the music of Roger Sessions, and the poetry of Richard Wilbur spring out of perversion resulting from the denial of sexuality? Surely this is to misread the part for the whole. But Mr. Fiedler is mysteriously reenforced by Mr. Charles Feidelson's *Symbolism and American Literature* (1953), a volume that haunts the classroom and the Modern Language Association. Perhaps the lesson of history is that history has no lesson, for the Western World has gone through this sort of thing twice before—once in the romantic movement of the eighteenth century and later, and again in mid-nineteenth-century Germany as a scholarly book has richly demonstrated—Dr. Lee Byron Jennings' remarkable study, *The Ludicrous Demon*, published in 1963.

I do not wish to be understood as saying that morality has disappeared from fiction but only that morality has been transmogrified. No such rational scheme as Kant's moral imperative or Jefferson's notion that man is endowed with a sense of right and wrong relative to society is acceptable to most novelists. There are, of course, exceptions. Harper Lee's *To Kill a Mockingbird* (1960) affirms the possibility of justice. James Gould Cozzens, in *The Last Adam,* wrote a story in which, amid casual fornication and insanity, democracy triumphs over typhoid germs, industrial selfishness, and medical hypocrisy. But in Hemingway a morally good act is one that makes you feel good afterwards, an interpretation that requires a prophetic capacity in individuals even more difficult to define than Jefferson's moral sense. In Faulkner the moral sense operates upside-down as outrage—things oughtn't to be that way, but they are—an idea not altogether new in the history of ethics. In many recent writers morality has no intellectual basis, but is referred to the emotions only, so that the reader is called upon to give his allegiance to pimps, thieves, prostitutes, failures, drunks, degenerates, sick and crazy personalities—in fact almost anybody not a member of the middle class. A later development of this aesthetic is that the novel, especially if it deal with frustration and degeneracy, will contain a cryptic symbolical figure who is the Christ. I have collected several variants of the Christ image imputed by critics to novels, including Huckleberry Finn, Joe Christmas in *Light in August,* Henry Fleming in *The Red Badge of Courage*—a book in which the sun pasted like a red wafer on the sky is not a mere vivid image but the eucharist—and Jay Gatz of Fitzgerald's *The Great Gatsby*. There seems to be also a vaguer school that attributes to Fitzgerald a desire to portray the Christ in Dick Diver of *Tender Is the Night* on the ground that he compassionately takes a great many sins upon his own psyche. This looks like a threat to psychiatrists.

Whatever the value of these symbolistic counters in the critical game, it is, I think, true that leading novelists in these latter days display either a hostility towards, or a profound suspicion of, human intelligence as

Jefferson understood intelligence: we deceive ourselves when we think
we think. Scientific research under this interpretation becomes therefore
a capacity of being perpetually well deceived. Precisely how, if the argument be true that logic and reason are the least of man's attributes, we
get along in commerce, diplomacy, social work, higher educational enter-
prises like the graduate school, medical research, civil rights, lawmaking,
chess playing, and the decisions of the Supreme Court is never quite made
clear, since, according to the premises, these and other exercises in testi-
mony, analysis, logic, proof, and judgment are either depraved, deceptive,
or egoistic—ego-projections is one term I have found—or all three.

iii

Into the vacuum created by their denial of Jeffersonian responsibility
the contemporary American novelists who count in criticism have thrust
forward two fallacies. One is the notion that an analysis of personality
problems is equivalent to the creation of character; and the other concerns the semantics of two nouns—"love" and "compassion." Let us examine these questions.

Like other great words "character" is a noun difficult to define, but
in the world's fiction either it has meant an eccentric personage, as when
one speaks of a humorous character in Smollett or says that Mr. Pickwick
is a typical Dickens "character"; or it refers to a quality of inner integrity,
latent or revealed but stable and confirmed, that results from education
in and through the world and arising from a considered view that life
is not mere emotion but existence involving philosophical and moral
values. Personality, on the other hand, is fleeting, pliant, fluid, indeter-
minate. We speak of a personality "disturbance," of personality "adjust-
ment," of personality "norms"; and even our inquiries about school
teachers, an occupation that requires, one would think, *some* inquiry
into character, commonly take shape as: "Do you know anything about
the applicant's personality that would unfit him for the position he is
applying for?"

Character grows from within; personality is altered, shaped, colored, influenced from without. We do not talk about character problems, though they are the great problems, but only about personality problems, which we think psychiatry can cure. Character is almost something given, like a landscape or the shape a rhinoceros has; personality, the novelist holds, can be altered by gimmicks like sex and disaster. In literature the great fictional names denote character—Ulysses, Don Quixote, Tom Jones, the Karamazov family, Faust, Hester Prynne, Uncle Tom, Isabel Archer.

In the modern novel sexuality may be more precisely delineated in a book like Styron's *Lie Down in Darkness* than it is in Dickens, but as somebody points out, no modern novelist has painted marital unhappiness more powerfully than does Dickens in *Dombey and Son,* where Mr. Dombey and Edith Granger live amid increasing tension. The great type of all our fantasies about erotic potency is Don Juan but in Byron's poem we see him in bed only twice, and in Mozart's opera not at all. The great figure of modern discontent with the conditions of mortality is Faust— so much so that Spengler in *The Decline of the West* says the Faustian spirit is the modern spirit, but our novelists will scarcely know what is meant if I say that Faust not only anticipated the frustrations and dark sexualities of their heroes and anti-heroes but also learned philosophy, coming in the end to accept the very civic responsibility the moderns find hollow. For the leading male personages in books by Saul Bellow, Paul Bowles, Jack Kerouac, Norman Mailer, James Purdy, and the rest, civic responsibility is a trap; but these writers perpetually brood over personality difficulties. They wish to express themselves. Their men and women therefore do not understand what is meant by character, they think the novelist, or God, or somebody else owes them a soul and that society should grant them perpetual felicity. But on mere personality no culture can be built. Novelists now take no responsibility for culture; they think it is the business of culture to take responsibility for novelists.

The second fallacy has to do with "love" and "compassion." Time was when publishers sold something called a "love story," meaning the kind of tale that, when it is transferred to the stage, we admire in plays as different as *As You Like It, The Barretts of Wimpole Street,* and *Guys and Dolls.* In the last fifty years we have had few love stories, sex having replaced the earlier noun and having become as mechanical in modern fiction as was the love story in the romance against which the modern novelist revolts. In English, unfortunately, "love" is a maid-of-all-work noun; and we find the moderns, who abolished love stories, nevertheless pleading for a general loving attitude on the part of the reader towards any personality they choose to present. This love is called "compassion" and is supposed to justify the presentation of even vicious and anti-social persons as central to life.

Like Alfred Kazin I am tired of reading for compassion instead of pleasure, and I heartily agree with Joseph Waldmeir that "perhaps indiscriminate compassion is a better description than universal love" for novelists who "seem intent on proving that all humanity is worthy of love by portraying the most unlovable in the sweetest terms." This is not merely a new form of sentimentality, it also displays ignorance of the meaning of compassion. Compassion is not general gush, it is an intellectual act accompanying an emotional interest. It is, as Edmund Fuller points out, not suspension of judgment, but the tempering and chastening of judgment, possible only because an anterior value system has been assumed. The famous statement: "There but for the grace of God go I" infers something called the grace of God, assumes that autonomy in the moral order has been granted to the speaker, and avers there is some trace of rationality in a universe in which God separates the object of compassion from the observer. True compassion is possible in the Jeffersonian world. The sentimental writer who implores pity for some poor devil because he has gone forth on a hopeless quest fails to understand that in the greatest novel about an insane man ever written, Don Quixote moves in a universe of rational values. When the modern novelist, lamenting anarchy and frustration, takes his manuscript to the modern publisher he really admits the same thing.*

This is perhaps a harsh remark. I have much sympathy with Harvey Swados' observation that "the novelist in America is not only negatively regarded as a man unfitted by background or training to contribute to the formation of intelligent attitudes on public affairs; he is positively regarded as a kind of freak unless he retreats to the university or hits the

---

* Lewis Mumford feels in much modern architecture the same disharmony between tenor and vehicle (to talk the language of modern criticism) that I find in much modern fiction. He writes of Frank Lloyd Wright's Guggenheim Museum: "If the outside of the building says Power—power to defy blast, to resist change, to remain as immune to time as the Pyramids—the interior says Ego, an ego far deeper than the pool in which Narcissus too long gazed. On the outside, Wright's composition put this architecture under the wing of the New Brutalist school; on the inside, he is the old Romanticist, singing—as if he were alone in the wilderness—the Song of Myself, but without communicating the sense of speaking for all other men and inviting their contributions and enhancing their personalities, too, that made Whitman's swelling ego so lovable." *The Highway and the City* (New York, The New American Library, 1964), p. 139.

jackpot in the mass media. Inevitably what he *does* also is regarded as freakish, unless his book strikes it rich." I say I have some sympathy with this remark, but my sympathy is limited. If the modern novelist really feels this way, he is himself mainly responsible for his own predicament. Brackenbridge, Charles Brockden Brown, Hawthorne, Cooper, Poe, William Gilmore Simms, Harriet Beecher Stowe, Albion W. Tourgee, Mark Twain, George W. Cable, Theodore Dreiser, Upton Sinclair, William Dean Howells, John Hay, William Allen White, and many other fictionists not only contributed to the formation of public attitudes but some of them occupied responsible government posts. I do not see that appointment as a writer in residence in a university is necessarily better than appointment as a consul in Venice or Liverpool. Indeed, the amount of self-pity among novelists seems to increase rather than diminish in proportion as prizes, foundations, fellowships, universities and college posts, writers' conferences, art colonies, public lectures, and jobs as publishers' readers, not to speak of paper-back reprints and textbook editions, multiply as plums that neither Cooper, Hawthorne, nor Henry James ever dreamed of. American society has not repudiated the novelist; the novelist has repudiated American society. As Mark Schorer has said, writers before the nineteenth century wished to reflect their age, writers in the nineteenth century wished to comfort their age, writers in the twentieth century wish to reject their age. I sometimes picture novelists and their critics living in a gigantic glass globe into which they ask us to peer but out of which they cannot see. They contemplate each other, not the rich, riotous, affirmative excitement of life.

iii

But as I am rapidly falling into a scolding mood, let me note that the daily papers pay a great deal of attention to the churches, institutions that delude millions of Americans into the belief that God governs life, and to the activities of one church in particular, which had at its head that great and good man, Pope John XXIII, and which has been laboring with an ecumenical council. One reads about the horrors of Nazi Germany; one also reads that Nazi Germany was destroyed by the very nations whose cynicism is the theme of many novels. One finds no trace of faculty psychology, but one does find an enormous interest in social altruism—great foundations, legislation for social security, present legislation for medicare, public interest in infancy and old age, something called the Peace Corps, students cheerfully going to jail in Mississippi to vindicate the rights of man. One reads of course about riots in the cities and at the summer resorts, but one discovers also that, judging by the marriage columns and the birth rate, most Americans believe in the family and in the future. One observes that the country takes some kinds of democratic action for granted—for example, the town meeting, the forum, the parent-teacher association, universal suffrage. It also spends billions of dollars on educational institutions which assume the young have rational minds, that these minds can be educated, and that skill is preferable to the lack of it. One who turns to the sports page notices how outraged Americans are when they discover a basketball fix—they seem to think some fundamental tenet of ethics is betrayed. One finds in the papers and in the news weeklies an enormous interest in science, which is, after all, the product of rationality, in the arts which have never been so widely supported as now, in cooking, health, gardening, vacation trips, the body beautiful, the proper rearing of children—topics that would have interested Socrates. Of course one will read that the press is unfair and inadequate (as it was in Jefferson's time), but one will reflect on the question whether distortion in the press is necessarily corrected by distortion in fiction. Why is one wrong, the other right?

The answer, apparently, is that the novel is a work of art, and a work of art is not to be judged as if it were a newspaper. Fair enough—but there remains that awkward figure of speech about the mirror moving down the road, and the lucid reflector of Henry James. I think it relevant to murmur something about a very great artist who also dealt in frustrations and atrocities but who saw life steadily and saw it whole. I infer that the practising novelist assumes that the only opposite he can envision to the novel is the novel of didacticism or the novel of propaganda. But this, surely, is naïve.

Novelists do not know enough. They speak and write brilliantly about craftsmanship, but they never quite face the question: when is a novel a work of art? *Huckleberry Finn* certainly expresses anxiety about American life, but it was written out of joyousness, not out of alienation. *The Portrait of a Lady* dramatizes egotism in Osmond and frustration in Isabel Archer, but the book is the product of an affirmative belief in human potentiality. *The Scarlet Letter* relates to an adulterous situation, but its three principals act like men and women, not like spoiled children.

In the atomic age there are a thousand things to be said against Jeffersonianism, but novelists have chosen the wrong things to say. The Jeffersonian belief in man is, I think, though darkened by time and trouble, still the basic belief of the Americans, who have repeatedly turned down attempts to establish a different form of society in the United States.

Technique is only a portion of art—an instrument, not an end. Under a wiser criticism than we now have, these gifted fiction-writers, monotonously repeating their variations on a limited number of themes, might find it possible to affirm man. "I believe," said William Faulkner, "that man will not merely endure, he will prevail." Faulkner gave him a soul capable of compassion, sacrifice and endurance, but Faulkner left out intelligence. Future novelists may yet return to accepting intelligence as essential in human nature and add to the democracy of the heart the democracy of the mind.* As George P. Elliott put it in *Harper's Magazine*

---

* After completing my manuscript I discovered the article by Gustav E. Mueller, "Philosophy in the Twentieth-Century American Novel," *The Journal of Aesthetics and Art Criticism*, 16(1):471–481 (June, 1948), which seems to reenforce my argument. Mueller notes the repudiation of Christianity by modern American novelists, their interpretation of economic life as mere greed for power, their repudiation of egalitarian democracy and of the idealism of moral freedom and rational responsibility. He thinks it valuable to learn from these novelists that "we must live together with what we call evil"—surely no new teaching—and seems to say that in exposing the "animal, subconscious, and inhibited impulses in human nature" the novelists, by exhibiting the dark brother of the self as in a mirror, are making a valuable contribution. So they are. But Mueller goes on to say that "a monism of the irrational is impossible, because irrational rebellions presuppose rational-moral standards, protesting against which the irrational *becomes* irrational." I think I follow this Hegelian dialectic, but with reference to Jeffersonianism it seems to lead us back precisely where we were, since if we are to have a rational democratic state we cannot found it on disguised irrationalism. Nor does Mueller make it quite clear to me, at least, how or where these novelists dramatize the conflict or confrontation between the dark mirror-image of the self and the public self of the individual.

That the artist may be completely "free" (i.e., beyond accepting any social responsibility whatsoever) is an interesting romantic thesis. But as Robert N. Wilson points out in the same journal ("Literature, Society, and Personality," 10(4):297–309, June, 1952) literature, being useful as an analytical or catalytic agent in understanding personality, also "acts upon the individuals of a society and thus may be viewed as a shaping force in personality, social structure, and culture," so that the writer cannot avoid some degree of social and public responsibility by merely denying it.

for May, 1965: "It is much too simple to think of society as nothing but the enemy of the individual and the artist, and it is much harder than any current liberal fashion allows for any individual, even an artist, not to be a member of society."

Confronting the celebrants of the powers of blackness and the writers of nihilistic fiction, and committed to the proposition that it cannot ignore the problems of contemporary society but must contribute what it can to their solution, what is the duty of education, of American humanism? The first thing to be said is that it is the duty of neither scholarship, nor criticism, nor teaching either to proscribe works of art or to prescribe to artists what they should write. That is the fashion in the dictator states. But scholarship, criticism, and teaching may properly judge what artists do.

The second thing to be said is that a wise humanism will view modernity, even the modernity of polymorphous sexuality and vehement declarations of alienation, with a certain sympathy based upon the truth that, as I have said, Western man has gone through all this before—in the literature of the Storm and Stress period, in the vast library of confessional writing that extends from St. Augustine through Rousseau to Henry Miller and William S. Burroughs. A wise teacher learns how to estimate what is truth and what is bluster in these documents.

In the third place it would be both fatuous and immoral for humanism to bid the artist be cheerful, write about nice people, compose pleasant music, paint pretty pictures, produce plays that are escape dramas only, and artificially infuse what he does with good humor.

In the fourth place—and here, I think, is the characteristic error of teaching and scholarship today—neither teaching nor scholarship (nor criticism!) should fall into the trap of interpreting the past only, or principally, in terms of current themes, present problems, and fashionable values. It should not, as it now tends to do, concentrate on Proust and Dostoevsky and Kierkegaard and the rest. There is also in the history of man something called serenity. Yet in the schools I think I could find twelve persons who have read *Oedipus Rex* for one person who has read *Oedipus Coloneus,* and for any twenty-five students steeped in D. H. Lawrence, I would scarcely find one who knows Goethe's maturer works.

The defence offered for the novel of violence is that the creator of the novel is not responsible for his theme or his values since his book merely reflects the violence of our time. But the purport of art is not merely to reflect, but to interpret, to select, to remold. Current critical theory seems to assume that the artist is merely a passive screen, and that, once he moves his mirror down the road or gazes into Henry James's large, lucid reflector, he performs his whole duty when he reports what he sees upon the surface of the mirror or the reflector. You cannot treat Shakespeare so. A wise teacher will glance from the novel to the totality of life it purports to reflect. He will ask how the novelist squares his assumption that the tragic flaw in American life is the irrationality of the soul with, let us say, the clean line of the great bridge that inspired Hart Crane, the incredible conquest of space in our time, our concern for integration and civil rights, our distress that poverty and ignorance are still far too widespread in the United States. These last are, I think, Jeffersonian considerations. I do not say they are themes for art or even for philosophy, but as components of American culture they lead me to doubt that American life is mainly frustration and insanity.

Irrationality and violence exist. But we shall have to leave to social scientists and historians the question whether, in proportion to the population, the incidence of violence and irrationality is greater now than formerly. A century and a half ago traveler after traveler was deeply disturbed by the illiteracy, lawlessness, and provincialism of the Americans. Then it was, however, that Dorothea Dix, appalled at the extent of insanity in the country and at the brutality with which it was treated, began her great reforms, and Dr. Isaac Ray, the first American psychiatrist, opened his distinguished career in Philadelphia. But though this leads the thoughtful student to question easy assertions about the incidence of violence and irrationality in contemporary America, it is to stray from the pedagogical point.

And what is that point? Simply, that the teacher fails to live up to his highest ethical obligations if he accepts uncritically current moral values and all the fashions of the present tense. The humanities exist to remind the artist that, although he has no duty to join any political party, he has a duty to recognize civil responsibility as a component of freedom. They also exist to remind readers that, however exciting the themes and the books of today, neither the themes nor the books are necessarily novel or eternal.

Is ours a violent world? So is the world in the historical books in the Bible, in the Homeric poems, in the Norse sagas, in Italian opera, in the fiction of Charles Dickens. Is human life threatened with extinction? So it is in the Buddhist doctrine of annihilation and recurrence, in the Christian anticipation of a Last Judgment that may come tomorrow, in the assumption of nineteenth-century scientists that the universe is running down to the terrible cold and darkness pictured in the last chapters of H. G. Wells's *The Time Machine*. Have men lost faith in God? In order? In justice? In the state? So had Job; St. Augustine; Jonathan Swift;

Goethe; Wordsworth; Carlyle, all of whom had the courage to think twice. Is the novelist alienated from a society too crass to comprehend his sensitivity? This was the complaint of Horace, Villon, Shakespeare in his sonnets, Beethoven, Thoreau, Rilke, Strindberg. Do the philosophical assumptions of Jefferson seem as outmoded as the psychological theory that gave him a rational faculty and a moral sense? Doubtless. But both the needs and the triumphs of human intelligence are still very great; and as for the moral sense, we do not need a Gallup poll and a computer to justify our feeling of outrage at what happened in Selma, Alabama. Are we threatened by atomic destruction? Yes. But anthropologists and pre-historians tell us of whole cultures destroyed by mysterious disease. In the fourteenth century most European countries, through the prevalence of the Black Death, lost from two-thirds to three-fourths of their population. We killed more persons in World War I and World War II in battle or by disease, starvation, and neglect than there were in the Roman Empire under Caesar Augustus. All this does not mean we should not take precautions against atomic destruction.

Those who do not know history are compelled to repeat history. But if the troubles of our proud and angry dust are from eternity and shall not fail, this cannot be construed to mean that the principal duty of the American novelist is to demand of his audience an indiscriminate pity for the unlovely population of his books. Pity is a good thing, sympathy is a good thing, but a better thing is courage based upon intelligence. Jefferson and even William Faulkner agree that man will survive.

NOTES

CHAPTER I—THE PROBLEM.

The passages cited from Herbert Croly may be found in the edition of *The Promise of American Life*, ed. Arthur M. Schlesinger, Jr., Cambridge, Massachusetts, 1965 (The John Harvard Library), pp. 33–34; 214; 409; 454. The passages cited from Bernard Rosenberg and David Manning White, *Mass Culture: The Popular Arts in America*, Glencoe, Illinois, 1957, are on pp. 5; 19–20.

CHAPTER II—THE ELEMENTS OF FICTION.

The most available edition of Charles Brockden Brown, *Alcuin: A Dialogue*, is that edited by LeRoy E. Kimball, New Haven, 1935. There is an edition of *Ormond* edited by Ernest Marchand, New York, 1937.

CHAPTER III—JEFFERSONIANISM.

The quotations from Jefferson may be found under appropriate names and dates in the *Writings of Thomas Jefferson*, 10 vols., ed. Paul Leicester Ford, New York, 1892–1889; and in *The Papers of Thomas Jefferson*, ed. Julian Boyd and others, Princeton, 1950–   , of which seventeen volumes have appeared, bringing the material down to November, 1790.

CHAPTER IV—THE CLASSICAL NOVEL BEFORE JAMES.

The *Works of J. Fenimore Cooper,* 12 vols., New York, 1849–1851, is known as the Author's Revised Edition. The Household Edition (*Works,* 32 vols., New York, 1876–1884) contains introductions to many of the novels by Susan Fenimore Cooper. The set most commonly found in 1895–1900.

Although a new, textually accurate edition of Hawthorne is now being published by the Ohio State University Press, pending its completion, one must use one of the standard "sets"—the *Complete Works of Nathaniel Hawthorne,* 12 vols., Boston, 1883 (the Riverside edition) or the *Complete Writings,* 22 vols., Boston, 1900. The passages I cite will of course be found under the appropriate titles in these (or other) editions. The passage on the "two Hawthornes" is borrowed in part from a piece written by Newton Arvin in 1929.

CHAPTER V—JAMES, HOWELLS, MARK TWAIN.

James's letter to Grace Norton is in the *Letters of Henry James,* 2 vols., ed. Percy Lubbock, New York, 1920, I:100–101. I have used the *Novels and Tales of Henry James,* 26 vols., New York, 1907–1917, the so-called New York edition. This has recently been reissued.

There is no collected edition of Howells. For my citations see his *Criticism and Fiction,* New York, 1891, pp. 95; 183–184; for the passages from *A Traveler from Altruria,* the Sagamore Press edition, New York, 1957, ed. H. M. Jones, p. 6; and for the passage from Howells' speech at the seventy-fifth birthday dinner, Everett Carter, *Howells and the Age of Realism,* Philadelphia, 1954, p. 193.

For passages cited from Mark Twain's "The Damned Human Race" see *Letters from the Earth,* ed. Bernard DeVoto, New York, 1962, pp. 17; 228–229. The citation from *The Mysterious Stranger,* New York, 1916, is on p. 140. The citations from Albert Bigelow Paine are from his *Mark Twain: A Biography,* 4 vols., New York, 1912, I:397; III:1157; 1297; 1469. There are several more or less standard collections of Mark Twain, none of them complete.

CHAPTER VI—YESTERDAY AND TODAY.

The sentence from *The Adventures of Augie March* by Saul Bellow, New York, 1953, is on p. 159. The sentence from *East of Eden* by John Steinbeck, New York, 1952, is on p. 217. I have forgotten where I picked up the sentence about Joel Knox in *Other Voices, Other Rooms*. The description of the rural constabulary may be found in Thomas Wolfe, *Of Time and the River*, New York, 1935, p. 369. The quotation from *A Farewell to Arms*, New York, 1929, is on p. 191. General Cummings's statement to Lieutenant Hearn is in Norman Mailer, *The Naked and the Dead*, New York, 1948, p. 82.

CHAPTER VII—CONCLUSION IN WHICH, PERHAPS, NOTHING IS CONCLUDED.

The description of Fiedler's *Love and Death in the American Novel* comes from Walter Sutton, *Modern American Criticism* [Princeton], 1963, p. 212. The article by Joseph Waldmeir from which I quote is "Quest without Faith," *The Nation* 193(17): November 18, 1961, pp. 390–396. The quotation from Harvey Swados is from "The Image in the Mirror" in *The Living Novel: A Symposium,* ed. Granville Hicks, New York, 1962 (Collier Books edition), p. 189. William Faulkner's *Speech of Acceptance upon the Award of the Nobel Prize for Literature* was published in a limited edition, New York, 1951, by the Spiral Press.